ENTER A SPY
The Double Life of Christopher Marlowe

Enter a Spy

THE DOUBLE LIFE OF CHRISTOPHER MARLOWE

by

Herbert Lom

MERLIN PRESS
LONDON

Illustrations by P. Kostal

Printed in Great Britain by A. Wheaton & Co. Ltd., Exeter

ISBN 0 85036 233 4

No portrait of Christopher Marlowe exists
nor any written description of him

Born: Canterbury, February 1564

Murdered: Deptford, May 30th 1593

To Alec

ACKNOWLEDGEMENTS

I would like to acknowledge the help of H.S., who wishes to remain anonymous in spite of the fact that without her literary and historical scholarship this volume could hardly have been prepared. I also acknowledge contributions from Patrick Brawn. Terry Eliot kindly lent a hand with the final editing of my text.

H.L.

FOREWORD

The violent, splendidly barbaric Elizabethan era, complete with brawls, murders, duels and normal and abnormal sexuality, attracted me ever since I spent some time in Cambridge studying the history of the theatre and the Elizabethan dramatists. I was fascinated by a period in which the Protestant-Catholic struggle dominated Europe in the way that the cold-war dominates our lives today. The same espionage organisations, the same witch-hunting and propaganda at work to make converts to one side or the other; the same pressure groups, racketeering and string-pulling.

One of the youngest but most expert string-pullers, double spy and tragic poet of genius, Kit Marlowe, became my hero long before today's anti-heroes "came in from the cold" and captured the imagination of the public.

Implicit in my subject matter and hinted at in my story is the Faust myth, the idea that Marlowe is Dr Faustus. Marlowe, like every writer, has echoed his own dilemma in his fictional work. Marlowe's vocation, his "better half" is the playwright-poet; his "shadow side" is the political and religious double-dealer, the betrayer, the spy. The Faust myth worked because in psychological terms Mephistopheles is an aspect of the Doctor, a "projection" of one aspect of his character, his materialistic ambition and his venality. Margaret, conversely, is "Anima" figure, the intuitive and inspirational virtue, the "love" principle. The characters around Marlowe (at least in the way I have arranged them) are interpretations of the Faust archetypes.

Another classic element of the Faust story is the same ingredient that exists in all tragedy since the Greeks: the idea of "the fatal flaw". It is often "hubris", the pride which so transcends wordly vanity that it challenges the gods themselves. Marlowe's character defect was a similar vice: cynicism and lack of commitment.

During the war I had some proof of the fact that actors often made the best agents and operators in enemy territory — for obvious reasons. The actor has developed techniques which involve believing what he is required to believe, seeing the other point of view — a kind of exercise in non-commitment to any single moral, political or religious identity. The actor inside the playwright Marlowe was what made him of value to his spy-masters. It is also the trait that seems to have led him progressively to early intercourse with the "Devil" of political intrigue and to betrayals he had not foreseen.

In the *Introduction* I give a factual account of Marlowe's life, character and literary output. My main story — the short story of a very short life — was written with the liberty of fiction, founded on the available facts about the poet's daring, dangerous, blundering career as a spy. I wrote it as a study for the preparation of a screen-play and, therefore, almost entirely in purely visual terms. In the use of language for my characters, I had the choice of basing it on Elizabethan prose, on Elizabeth the First's own speeches or on how we speak today. Because I lack the courage of a more gifted author, but also for other reasons, I did not attempt to re-create the elaborate charms of Elizabethan English but chose the language of today.

Roquebrune — Cap Martin, France.
June 1978.   H.L.

INTRODUCTION

No portrait of Marlowe exists, nor any written description of him. Yet he stands out as a vivid personality. He can be summed up as a fiery intellectual, a scholar-poet, an atheist at a time when atheism was a form of high treason; fearless and reckless in his opinions; a bohemian, an individualist who had to go his own way, his mind always restless and enquiring and questioning; a man who, in an age jostling with writers seeking patronage and with careerists angling for preferment, kept his own peculiar integrity; a man who founded his friendships mainly on intellectual companionship and common intellectual interests. Sir Walter Raleigh was one such friend; Thomas Harriott, Raleigh's mathematical tutor and scientist, was another; George Chapman, poet and translator of Homer, another of the same group—a group held together by a passionate interest in the growing points of scientific and philosophical thought, of geographical and astronomical discovery, and in the discussion of the foundations of religious belief. It was the climate of thought in which Giordano Bruno, Keppler and Galileo were also living.

Marlowe never married, and no woman figures in his life. Emotional love, in its physical expression, was probably unimportant to him. His mind teemed with learning, with legend, with imaginative vision which he had the power to express in words. He was intoxicated by language, the language of his own tongue and that of the Romans and Greeks; by the sensuousness of sound. His mind speculated endlessly on man's capacity to transcend human limitations, on the power and the limits of knowledge; it moved forward to the frontiers of science and back to the pagan classics. It was his intellectual passion that gave him his fundamental emotional experiences — and these he could share only with men.

"All they that love not tobacco and boys are fools," he is recorded as saying, and the impatient rationality of this remark has the sound of his own voice.

As might be expected, his enemies — those who disliked his opinions or were jealous of his talent — were also articulate. Robert Greene, Gabriel Harvey and Thomas Kyd were among those who denigrated him — as a "vaine-glorious Tragedian" out-braving better pens with "the swelling bumbast of bragging blanke verse", and as a "hawty man" who admired nothing but "his wondrous selfe," "intemperate and of a cruel harte", "arrogant and conceited." But these are the usual brick-bats flung at the exceptionally gifted by the also-rans.

On this view of Marlowe's personality — especially his cast of mind, and the relative unimportance to him of women — it is exceedingly difficult to imagine him as the main author of some of the Shakespearean plays in which the convincing observation of women plays a part. In Marlowe's six plays (*Tamburlaine, Doctor Faustus, The Jew of Malta, Edward II,* and the minor *Massacre at Paris* and *Dido Queen of Carthage*) the women have a small and conventional place in his essentially masculine drama. They are women imported from literary sources. The language of love (Tamburlaine to Zenocrate, Faustus to Helen) is literary hyperbole — magnificent but not realistic as in the Shakespearean love scenes. The erotic *Hero and Leander* is also literary in its inspiration. Marlowe makes none of the perceptive discoveries of female character and behaviour that we get for example in Helena and Hermia, Beatrice, Rosalind and Celia, Viola.

2

Marlowe was fascinated by the writings of Machiavelli. No picture of Marlowe's cast of mind can be complete without recognising the influence worked upon his imagination by the writings of this Florentine political philosopher who had died about fifty years before Marlowe became a student, and whose works, now becoming available in England, were shocking and fascinating the students of his day. In the *Jew of Malta*, Marlowe makes 'Machiavel' the prologue-speaker, and gives him words that seem to speak, under-cover as it were, for Marlowe himself:

"I count religion but a childish toy,
And hold there is no sin but ignorance."

And later —

"Many will talk of titles to a crown;
What right had Caesar to the empery?
Might first made kings, and laws were then most sure
When, like the Draco's, they were writ in blood" —

— here, at any rate, is a declaration of interest which may indeed have led Marlowe to the studies of Richard III and Richard II, and (to be blindly tendentious) to the central problems of Julius Caesar, Coriolanus, Macbeth and Lear. Apart from Prospero the Faustian, it is also possible to see Iago as the perfect poor man's Machiavelli; and to see Hamlet (a graduate of the same university, Wittenberg, as Faustus) as the Scholar-Prince who at a court where the spilling of blood had made a king, was ineffective and impotent in the face of power seized on Machiavellian principles.

It is possible to see all the dead kings of the histories descended from Tamburlaine —

"Oft have I levelled, and at last have learned
That peril is the chiefest way to happiness.
What glory is there in a common good
That hangs for every peasant to achieve?
That like I best that flies beyond my reach." —

—which in turn can be taken as the epitaph of the protagonists of the tragedies. In fact, if one really put one's mind to it, one could find some expression of Marlowe's mind in most of the Shakespearean histories and tragedies.

Before looking at the shadowy facts of Marlowe's life, it is necessary to appreciate some essential background facts with which his life was linked. Having seen the kind of intellectual he was — radical, fearless, with all knowledge as his province; and with the problems of power, intellectual and monarchical, alive in his imaginataion — we can further see him as the type of man who was bound to get caught up in the ideological struggle of his time. In this respect he becomes an extraordinarily modern character. The Protest-ant-Catholic struggle that dominated Europe in his lifetime has many parallels in the cold war of recent times, and this background of our own times is useful in helping us to enter imaginatively into Marlowe's.

On the individual plane there was the same concealment or open declaration of sympathies, the same espionage organisations and the amassing of political intelligence by both sides at home and abroad; the same witch-hunting, the same forces of propaganda at work to make converts to one side or the other, and the same attempt to protect minorities stranded in the enemy camp — as, for example, the attempts of the English ambassador in Paris to obtain assurances of protection for the French Protestants, and conversely, the steady escape of English Catholics into foreign asylum. It has been estimated that Protestant refugees from Europe who were in London in the 1580's included three thousand from the Low Countries, five hundred from France, and one hundred and forty from Italy.

During Marlowe's lifetime, this struggle became crystal-lised in two major national events: first, in 1587 when he was twenty-three, the execution of Mary Queen of Scots, considered to be the focus of Catholic intrigue at home, the "fifth column" that was a treacherous danger to the life of Queen Elizabeth and the security of the realm. Secondly, in the following year 1588, came the defeat of Catholic Spain's Armada. England, in effect, was busy consolidating its Protestant revolution, and at home it showed no mercy in the process. Protestant unorthodoxy was not tolerated, and men who held so-called heretical opinions—God-fearing as they might be—paid with their lives.

It is worth mentioning that a young Clergyman Francis Kett, whose residence at Corpus Christi College, Cambridge, overlapped with Marlowe's, was burned at Norwich in 1589 for his Unitarian views: Matthew Hamont of Hethersett, a God-fearing playwright who chose not to take the Bible literally, had been burned ten years earlier in the same place; and by 1587, the year Marlowe left Cambridge, four more simple and sincere men had gone up in flames in Norwich and nearby for *Protestant* unorthodoxies that the realm could ill afford to have ventilated at this stage of its struggle. (The intolerance of the "consolidation" period of a revolution again has obvious parallels in our own time.)

Patriotism was equated with Protestantism. Atheism, therefore, was worse than a heresy; it was also high treason. It was also, however, a very difficult form of heresy to prove.

The first intimation that Marlowe was swimming in deep waters comes from the extraordinary circumstances in which he was awarded his Master of Arts degree at Cambridge University in 1587, at the age of 23.

A word must be said here about the sources of facts for Marlowe's life. Many of the facts on which recent biography and criticism rests (a fairly small body of work), have been painstakingly uncovered in the last fifty years* or so from

* By Dr. Leslie Hotson, F. S. Boas, John Bakeless and others.

official and legal documents, state records, university and college records, and official MSS. Marlowe's life is lived partly in shadow, partly in the sudden and dramatic light that these discoveries throw on him. The facts given in this account are therefore the "assumed" biographical facts, based either on the direct evidence, or on reasonable deductions that have been made from the evidence. Where only "theory" can exist, this is indicated. There is incidentally no satisfactory biography of Marlowe yet; the few in existence concentrate on the more sensational discoveries and are particularly weak, for example, in the history of the theatre-companies with which he was associated.

Marlowe arrived at Corpus Christi College, Cambridge, at the end of 1580, aged 16 or 17, on a scholarship awarded from the King's School, Canterbury. He was expected to read for holy orders. The Chancellor of the University was the Queen's first minister and Lord Treasurer, Lord Cecil of Burleigh, who kept in close touch with University affairs. The University at that time consisted of 14 colleges and about 1700 students. Wealthy students and the sons of noblemen entered as "fellow commoners". The bulk of the students were, like Marlowe, pensioners. The poorest were sizars who worked their way through college by doing boot-cleaning, waiting at table and other menial tasks. Among the wealthy students contemporary with Marlowe were Burleigh's son Robert Cecil (who eventually succeeded his father as the mainstay of the Queen's government); and Burleigh's ward, the 14-year-old Earl of Essex, at Trinity in Marlowe's first year. Among the budding dramatists later to be grouped with Marlowe as the "University Wits" were Thomas Nashe, in residence as a sizar; and Robert Greene, an M.A. of 1584. The administrative head of Marlowe's own College, Corpus, was Robert Norgate, a master with strong puritanical leanings who had gathered about him a group of dons with much the same views.

The Cambridge scholarship accounts record regular weekly payments to Marlowe (the scholarship was worth a shilling a week) up to the time he was accorded his first degree (Bachelor of Arts) in 1584 — except for an apparent absence of seven weeks in the spring of 1583 (in spite of the fact that the terms of his scholarship forbade any scholar to leave Cambridge for more than a month). His position among the B.A.'s of his year was 199th out of 231; among the B.A.'s of Corpus, he was 8th. In spite of this indifferent record, however, his scholarship was renewed for a further three years for his higher degree. His absences from Cambridge now became much more frequent, from the records of the Bursar's account and the Buttery Book of Corpus. He always appears to be spending more money than he is drawing. In the first term of the new academic year he drew only three weeks' scholarship money, in the second term seven and a half weeks', in the third term four weeks', and so on. The following year his absences total about four months. The year after, he seems to have been present nine and a half weeks in the first term, and just over five in the second.

Such was his record when in March 1587 he made his formal application for his M.A. degree to the Master and Fellows of Corpus: —

> "Christopher Marley* petitions your reverences that the nine
> full terms (after his completing the last) in which he has
> followed the ordinary lectures (even if not wholly in
> accordance with the form of statute) together with all the
> opponencies, responsions and the other exercises required
> by royal statute, may suffice for him to commence in arts."

* This was his usual way of writing his name. Other variations are Morley, Marlin, Merling, Marle, Marlowe.

This was the usual form of application; even so, the "nine full terms" was an optimistic reckoning, to say the least. From the remarkable sequel, it is assumed that the University authorities were unwilling to admit Marlowe to his degree; otherwise the Queen's Privy Council would not have intervened, as it did three months later. At its meeting of 29th June 1587, the Privy Council minuted a resolution referring to the rumours and reports concerning Christopher Morley, certifying that he had served his Queen well and deserved to be rewarded; and requesting that he should be allowed to proceed with his degree. The text as it stands in the Minutes of the Privy Council is as follows: —

> "Whereas it was reported that Christopher Morley was determined to have gone beyond the seas to Reames (Rheims) and there to remaine, their Lordships thought good to certify that he had no such intent, but that in all his actions he had behaved himself orderly and discreetly whereby he had done her Majesty good service, and deserved to be rewarded for his faithful dealing. Their Lordships' request was that the rumour thereof should be allayed by all possible means, and that he should be furthered in the degree he was to take this next commencement; Because it was not her Majesty's pleasure that anyone employed as he had been in matters touching the benefit of his country should be defamed by those who are ignorant in th'affairs he went about."

Two days later Marlowe was granted his degree — or more accurately, he had wrested it from the teeth of the grimly disapproving dons who had recently washed their hands of him. The whole episode must have been enormously satisfying. It will be remembered that one of the Queen's Privy Councillors was Burleigh, not only Lord Treasurer, but also Chancellor of Cambridge University. Another of them was the Queen's Secretary of State, Sir Francis Walsingham, organiser-in-chief of the secret service, and cousin to the Thomas Walsingham of Chislehurst, Kent—later on, if not already, Marlowe's friend and patron. These are the bare facts of Marlowe's six years at Cambridge. What can be made of them?

Since the discovery of the Privy Council document, it has been generally accepted that Marlowe had been acting as a secret government agent during his years at Cambridge—possibly from 1583 or 1584 onwards, at a time when the Protestant-Catholic struggle was becoming increasingly critical. The actual implications of the document were fairly clear: that during his time at Cambridge, Marlowe had been employed at the highest level "in matters touching the benefit of his country": that he was the subject of gossip and rumour in the university; that he was rumoured to have gone to Rheims—the site of the well-known seminary of English Catholic students—and had thus been "smeared" for Catholic sympathies, the very reverse of the truth; and that people who didn't know what they were talking about had better keep quiet.

His absences can thus be accounted for, either on his missions abroad, or on visits to London to receive his instructions. It is not known, however, how he got involved in this work, or who his Cambridge political contacts could have been. No convincing theories have been put forward. If one had to produce a theory, however, it would almost certainly lead back to Sir Francis Walsingham.

The outline of Sir Francis Walsingham's career is well authenticated. He was always a fanatical Protestant. He had been appointed Secretary of State by Queen Elizabeth in 1572 (when he was aged about 42), and held that position until his death in 1590. With Burleigh, he shared most of the administrative responsibilities of government, with special responsibility for foreign affairs. In the service of a despotic queen, however, his freedom of action was limited. He concentrated on getting political information, and devoted a large part of his private fortune to maintaining an efficient espionage system. At one time he was known to have in his pay at least 53 private agents placed in France, Germany, the Low Countries, Italy, Spain and Turkey. He himself had undertaken various diplomatic missions abroad, and on one such mission (to Paris, in 1581) he entertained his future son-in-law, Philip Sidney, and another poet (later to be Marlowe's friend) Thomas Watson.

Between 1583 and 1586 (the years of Marlowe's probable activity), Walsingham was putting all possible pressure on the Queen to intervene on behalf of the Protestants in the Low Countries against the Spanish armies; it is well known that he despaired of getting the vacillating Elizabeth to make up her mind, and we may imagine that he therefore redoubled his efforts to get the kind of political intelligence that would convince her. Marlowe, then, may have been one of the agents he enlisted for this critical period. In 1583 Walsingham's daughter Frances married Philip Sidney. In 1585 Walsingham's untiring pressure on the Queen produced an apparent result: he was allowed to negotiate with the Dutch Commissioner in London the terms on which the Queen was willing to make war on Spain in the Low Countries. At the end of the same year, however, the Earl of Leicester was more successful in getting the Queen to approve of direct intervention: he engaged the Spaniards in the Low Countries with his expedition of six thousand men; his nephew, Philip Sidney, fell in battle the following October, in 1586. (It may be added that Walsingham's daughter, Philip's widow, later married the young Earl of Essex.) Walsingham's spies were, however, being active on another front at the same time; on the basis of their reports he was able to unmask the Babington plot and to secure the conviction of Mary Queen of Scots for high treason in October 1586 (the same month in which Sidney died). Under his further pressure, Elizabeth reluctantly overcame her scruples about the execution, which took place on 8th February 1587; in the same year, his agents in Spain were busy informing him of Spanish preparations for a naval expedition; and again, in the same year, he and his fellow Privy Councillors made their exceptional intervention on Marlowe's behalf with the Cambridge authorities.

Marlowe's activities must therefore fit somewhere into this background. But there are a few further points to note. It is possible, in theory, that Walsingham also had his own agents or security men planted in the Universities, and that one such agent was Marlowe's original contact. From Walsingham's point of view, the universities would have been obvious places to keep under observation. They were closely linked with the established church. Masters and fellows were all in holy orders. The colleges existed mainly to provide an educated and orthodox clergy for the future, and Walsingham may have considered it his business to make sure that they bred no secret unortho- doxies or under-cover Catholics.

Marlowe, then, may have gone to Rheims, to pick up information at the English Catholic college, or to the Low Countries, or both; in either case as a genuine divinity student, garbed accordingly. At the same time he may well have been acting as some kind of agent-provocateur on Walsingham's behalf, provoking his fellow divinity students to indicate their sympathies one way or another by expressing pro-Catholic sentiments himself. This would explain the rumours to which the Privy Council refers, and would also account for the refusal of the University authorities to grant an absentee Catholic suspect his higher degree. But whether or not his "double-talk" was deliberate, we can imagine him enjoying it hugely as he became more and more bored with his formal studies (as his B.A.

11

position indicates), and more and more irritated by the
pious orthodoxy of his fellow students (Francis Kett
excepted). His imagination was already fired by all the
reading he was doing off the syllabus; he was doing verse
translations of Ovid and Lucan; the Aeneid was turning his
thoughts to a play, and the story of Tamburlaine was
seething in his mind; the doctrines of Machiavelli, cynical
and amoral, excited and stimulated him. All religion,
protestant or not, was becoming irrelevant — with orthodoxy
a device of policy, and the servants of God anything but
God-like in their conduct.

At the time, however, those who secretly used him knew
him only as a ferocious anti-Catholic; they could not
possibly have used anyone suspected of atheism. Later,
when such suspicions against Marlowe hardened, he became
a danger to them. His loyalty could no longer be counted
on, and he knew far too much. It is almost certainly as a
direct, or indirect consequence of this fact that he met his
death — or disappeared — in 1593.

Some time in the summer of 1587, Marlowe settled in
London — it is not known where exactly, except that he was
living in the Liberty of Norton Folgate, adjoining Finsbury
Fields, two years later. There is no evidence that he left the
country or travelled far afield from London in the
remaining years. There are few dates to go on. It is not
even known in what order he wrote the plays. *Tamburlaine*
is the only one that was actually published in his lifetime
(in 1590). All the plays were of course *acted* in his lifetime,
but it was the usual practice not to publish a play while it
was still "alive" in the theatre, for a variety of good
commercial reasons. The rage for *Tamburlaine*, his first
London production (1587), had thus presumably abated by
1590, and publication of the text could be permitted. His
other plays, however, as we know, were still running up to
1595, the year after his death. There is no evidence at all

that Marlowe and Shakespeare ever met. It is assumed that they "must" have met, partly because London was only the size of a provincial town today (about 150,000-200,000 inhabitants), and that all the theatre writers "must" have known each other. Marlowe however in, say, 1590 was already the leading tragedian of his day, and Shakespeare, at best, was a provincial apprentice in the theatre. Various critics again assume that they "must" have met in order to work over bits of Henry VI together, if not Richard III and other texts in which the hands of both Marlowe and Shakespeare (and others) are discernible. Against this largely negative background, we can now summarise the probable character of Marlowe's professional and private life, at the same time keeping an eye on the links with the Shakespeare plays.

Tamburlaine was acted in the year that Marlowe came down from Cambridge, 1587, and was an immediate and phenomenal success mainly because it was the first blank verse play that wasn't utterly dreary. It is probable that he started work on it while he was still at Cambridge—the material for it was in the University Library—and that he already had contacts in London from his other activities before he actually settled there. The title role was almost certainly taken by "Star" Edward Alleyn, acting at The Theatre, Shoreditch (on the way to Finsbury Fields, north of the road from London Bridge). This Theatre had been built by James Burbage in 1576. It was the first permanent theatre in England, and the only one at that time, as its name indicates. Alleyn remained Marlowe's chosen interpreter; and when Alleyn quarrelled with Burbage in 1591-2 he removed himself and some of his Company (the Lord Admiral's) to a rival theatre that had been built in 1587 by Philip Henslowe. This was the Rose, Bankside, south of the river. Marlowe's plays went with him, and the rivalry of the two managements, Henslowe's and Burbage's,

13

started. By 1593, some of Alleyn's old company returned to the Burbage theatre (now in the hands of the two sons, Cuthbert and Richard), with Richard Burbage their leading actor and Alleyn's chief rival. They were now nominally the Chamberlain's men, and Shakespeare was among them as an actor in 1594. By that year Marlowe was dead.

To return to the events after the first production of *Tamburlaine*, there is no biographical information connected with the writing of the remaining plays, except contemporary allusions to them. As I have already noted, all Marlowe's plays are *first* plays, not based on earlier ones like so many of Shakespeare's. *Doctor Faustus* is assumed to have followed in 1588; the *Jew of Malta* in about 1589; *Edward II* in about 1592. Thereafter they were continually played in Henslowe's repertory, at the Rose Theatre, though *Edward II* is probably the only one that actually had its first performance there; the others were written while Alleyn was still playing for Burbage.

Two minor plays, *The Massacre at Paris* and *Dido Queen of Carthage*, are so inferior that it is difficult to regard them, as is usually done, as coming after *Edward II*. The Massacre belongs, in content, to Marlowe's more orthodox Protestant period, describing as it does the Massacre of St. Bartholomew—the slaughter of the French Protestants which had taken place in 1572 when he was a boy. The violent Protestant sentiments are hardly worthy of the latter-day Marlowe. It may well be that he drafted it at Cambridge—it is altogether rather under-graduate, including the lengthy discussions of the rival logical systems of Aristotle and Petrus Ramus—and then brought it up to date to be acted a year or so before his death; if so, the loyal sentiments would have been a useful "public front" to offset the increasing rumours about his atheism. *Dido* was published the year after his death, 1594, with

14

both his and Thomas Nashe's names on the title page; and it is interesting that this is the only play of Marlowe's that attempts to present a heroine, and the only one in which a collaborator is named. It was probably drafted while they were both at Cambridge, or soon after their arrival in London. Nashe was a common friend of Marlowe's and Robert Greene's; the three of them had been at Cambridge together and were all writing for the theatre. Greene, however, the oldest and most rakish, was so envious of Marlowe and everyone else more successful than himself that they were not a trio in a personal sense, although they are often judged (on textual grounds) to have co-operated professionally. There is a good deal of information about the literary slanging matches in which Greene especially indulged, and about the professional jealousies that abounded. Greene died of dissipation in 1592, and is usually credited with the first allusion to Shakespeare's presence in London (the "upstart crow" passage) in the book of his confessions published shortly after his death.

Nashe and Greene, together with Thomas Kyd, were among the more prominent of Marlowe's bohemian and somewhat raffish professional colleagues. His closest friends were more or less outside the hectic jungle-life of the theatre, though occasionally they were drawn into it. There is a well-documented account, for example, of the street fight in which Marlowe and his studious friend Thomas Watson were involved in September 1589. This is one of the few actual incidents in Marlowe's life which is recorded in some detail; there are in fact only about two others — a brush with some constables, which came to nothing; and the account of his death. All three incidents are preserved in police court records.

Thomas Watson, like all Marlowe's London friends, arrived in his life without any evidence to show how he got there. The fight involved a young man called William

Bradley, who for complicated reasons had a grudge against both Watson and Marlowe. Bradley and Marlowe, meeting apparently by chance on the road towards Finsbury Fields and the Theatre (where *The Jew of Malta* may have been running) got involved in a sword-and-dagger fight. Thomas Watson came up, and Bradley thereupon let up on Marlowe, to attack his second enemy. Marlowe stood back. In the bitter struggle that followed, Thomas Watson was forced to give Bradley a mortal wound in the effort to save his own life. Both he and Marlowe were arrested. Marlowe spent a few days in Newgate Prison and was allowed out on bail until the trial two months later. Watson, however, spent the two months in Newgate. Marlowe was exonerated at the trial (held at the "Olde Bailie"), and Watson, having been judged to have killed in self-defence, was returned to prison to await the Royal pardon, which arrived some three months later.

Marlowe's relations with Thomas Kyd also have importance, since Kyd was both a professional colleague and was charged with political conspiracy at the time Marlowe was also getting into serious difficulties. Some time in 1591, the two men were in Kyd's words, "writing in one chamber" together. This may have been about the same time Kyd was writing his famous *Spanish Tragedy*; Marlowe may have started on Edward II or one of the "Shakespeare" histories. Kyd was about 33 at this time, some six years older than Marlowe. Unlike the other professional playwrights, he was not a university man but a scrivener—a drafter of letters or documents, or possible secretary to a nobleman.

It may be convenient here to give the gist of the depositions which Kyd made against Marlowe in 1593 just after Marlowe was dead. Referring to his life with Marlowe, Kyd says: "It was his custom when I knew him first, and as I hear say he continued it in table talk and otherwise, to jest at the divine scriptures, gibe at prayers, and strive in argument to frustrate and confute what hath been spoke by prophets and such holy men." There is more in the same vein, with specific examples, including highly scandalous assertions about the personal relations of St. John the Evangelist and Jesus Christ! All this came out later, when Kyd was trying to clear himself of "guilt by association" with Marlowe, and was trying to prove that some so-called atheistic papers found in his room were in fact Marlowe's (now safely dead), but that they had been "shuffled with some of mine, unknown to me, by some occasion of our writing in one chamber two years since." Whatever Kyd's true relations with Marlowe were—whether or not an initial sympathy with his views turned to later panic and recantation—it nevertheless appears that they had known each other for some time, were in fact writing for the same nobleman's company of players at some stage, and had shared a room or workroom together for a period.

The most renowned of Marlowe's friends was Sir Walter Raleigh. Again we do not know how their paths first crossed. Marlowe's six years in London coincided with some well-known events in Raleigh's life—his appointment in 1587 as Captain of the Queen's Guard; the Earl of Essex's arrival at Court in the same year, and the threat to Raleigh's supremacy as Queen's favourite; the visit to Ireland in which he brought back the poet Spenser and the first three books of the Faery Queen (from which Marlowe quotes); his disgrace in 1592 when he was cast into the Tower ostensibly for "wronging" one of the Queen's Maids of Honour, Elizabeth Throckmorton, who became his wife; and finally the dark rumours of irreligion which gathered about his and Marlowe's name in 1593 and 1594. In Raleigh's circle—whose headquarters were presumably Durham House, the Strand—were Thomas Harriott or Herriot, mathematician and astronomer; Henry Percy, the ninth Earl of Northumberland (later a fellow prisoner with Raleigh in the Tower), Walter Warner, another mathematician; George Chapman, poet and classicist and later a writer for the theatre; and Matthew Roydon, another (now forgotten) poet. These are the people usually referred to, with Marlowe, in the Raleigh circle.

A pamphlet published by an English Jesuit in Rome in 1593 referred to "Sir Walter Rawley's School of Atheism" wherein "both Moses and our Saviour, the Old and the New Testaments, are jested at, and the scholars taught among other things to spell God backwards." However ill-informed and tendentious the pamphlet may have been, it did however indicate the extent of public gossip. Further information was lodged with the authorities during the first half of the same year by one Richard Baines (about whom nothing more is known). Baines's statement, the full text of which exists, is headed "A Note containing the opinions of one Christopher Marley concerning his damnable judgment of religion, and scorn of God's word." It is a collection of reported sayings of Marlowe's. These include "that Moses was but a juggler and that one Heriots (Harriott) being Sir W. Raleigh's man can do more than he"; "that the first beginning of Religion was only to keep men in awe"; that the New Testament is "filthily written"; and many personal aspersions of New Testament characters on the same lines as those reported by Kyd. In addition, "one Ric. Cholmley hath confessed that he was persuaded by Marlowe's reasons to become an Atheist." The same Cholmley is further reported to have spoken "all evil of the (Privy) Counsell, saying thay they are all Atheists and Machiavellians, especially my Lord Admiral," and—regretting that he had not killed the Lord Treasurer (Burleigh)—that "he could never have done God better service". Lastly, "this Marlowe not only holds all these opinions himself, but into almost every company he cometh he persuades men to atheism, willing them not to be afraid of bugbears and hobgoblins, and utterly scorning both God and his ministers, as I Richard Baines will justify and approve both by mine oath and the testimony of many honest men, and almost all men with whom he hath conversed any time will testify the same."

This is a sweeping claim, and presumably the authorities thought something ought to be done about it. While Baines was making this statement, or shortly before, Thomas Kyd's room was being searched. Papers which he passed off as Marlowe's were seized; he himself was arrested on ground of political conspiracy and put to the torture. The seized papers were later identified as a vehement Unitarian argument, extracted from an old book. This is an interesting reminder of the Unitarian heretic, Francis Kett, Marlowe's fellow student.

During these events, Marlowe was probably out of London, staying and working at Thomas Walsingham's manor at Scadbury, in the parish of Chislehurst, Kent; because evidently the Privy Council knew where to find him. The plague epidemic that had broken out the previous year meant that theatre activities were fitful, there was practically no market for new plays, and various companies had gone into the provinces with old ones. His last (attributed) play was *Edward II*, written a year or so before. On 18th May 1593, however, he received a summons from the Privy Council. It issued "a warrant to Henry Maunder, one of the messengers of Her Majesty's chamber, to repair to the house of Mr. Thomas Walsingham in Kent or to any other place where he shall understand Christopher Marlowe to be remaining and by virtue thereof to apprehend and bring him to the Court in his company, and in case of need to require aid." Some weeks earlier, similar proceedings had been taken against Richard Cholmley and one Richard Strange. Two days after the issue of the warrant, the Privy Council records that "This day Christopher Marley of London, Gent, being sent for by warrant from their Lordships hath entered his appearance accordingly for his indemnity therein, and is commanded to give his daily attendance on their Lordships until he shall be licensed to the contrary." (Among the changes of the Privy Council since their first formal intervention in Marlowe's life, were the loss of Sir Francis Walsingham, who had died three years before, in 1590; and the recent appointment by the Queen of the Earl of Essex; he was then 26.) With that the whole matter vanishes from the records, and a few days later Marlowe was dead.

The official version of Marlowe's death was given to the Coroner's Jury by Ingram Frizer, the man who killed him. With Frizer were two others: Robert Poley and Nicholas Skeres. Both Ingram Frizer and Robert Poley have been traced through the records. Frizer is alluded to in legal documents of the time as "Thomas Walsingham's man", and long after the incident he continued to do business for the Walsingham family. He seems to have been in and out of the lawcourts on various business matters, including a matter of issuing fraudulent bonds in his master's name. In later life, after retirement, he apparently became a churchwarden and tax collector in Kent. Robert Poley was also a "Walsingham man", and a known government secret agent; many of his ciphers, letters and reports survive. If he is identifiable with the Robert Pollye who matriculated as a sizar of Clare College, Cambridge, in 1568, he could be seen as a tenuous connecting link between Marlowe's Cambridge and London lives. He is known to have been spying for Francis Walsingham in connection with the Babington plot, but his part in it was so involved that he may have been spying for both the Protestant and Catholic sides at once. At any rate his methods were dark and devious to a degree. Nicholas Skeres figures only as a corroborating witness of Frizer's evidence.

Frizer's evidence, as accepted by the Coroner's Jury, was as follows: About ten o'clock in the forenoon of 30th May 1593, he, Marlowe, Poley and Skeres met together at Deptford "in a room in the house of a certain Eleanor Bull, widow, and there passed the time together & dined & after dinner were in quiet sort together & walked in the garden until the sixth hour after noon & then returned from the garden to the room & there together and in company supped". After supper, Frizer continues, he and Marlowe had an argument about the payment of the bill. Marlowe was lying on a bed; Frizer was near the bed, with his back to it, and with his body facing the table. Poley and Skeres were on either side of him, sitting at the table, so that he could not get up. Marlowe, moved with anger about the argument he and Frizer had been having, thereupon suddenly drew Frizer's dagger, which was at his back, and gave him two head wounds, two inches long and a quarter of an inch deep. Frizer, penned between Poley and Skeres, could not get away from Marlowe; he wrenched the dagger from him, in defence of his life, and gave Marlowe a mortal wound above the eye, two inches deep and one inch wide, "of which mortal wound the afore-said Christopher Morley then and there instantly died."

Marlowe was killed on Wednesday evening, May 30th 1593. The inquest was held on Friday, June 1st. His body could not be buried until the coroner's jury had viewed it; but it was taken to the Church of St. Nicholas, Deptford, the same day and buried probably in the churchyard. Frizer and his companions were all pardoned, after the usual formalities. The Coroner happened to be "William Danby, Coroner of the Household of our said Lady the Queen"—since Deptford was within twelve miles of the Sovereign's person.

The story of Marlowe's life and death is like an uncompleted detective story. Clues have been patiently uncovered and followed up, but they leave a multitude of key questions unanswered. And no one has yet been able to answer the obvious questions arising from Frizer's account of the death; why was Marlowe spending the day with these unlikely companions? Why were three men unable to overpower and disarm one man without killing him? Why did they all seek the privacy of Eleanor Bull's room and garden from ten in the morning until after dark? Briefly, three theories are possible:

(i) The straightforward explanation: Marlowe was being warned by the Privy Council to keep quiet. If they had been more worried about him, they could have put him under arrest without more ado, like Kyd. As a result of his daily attendance on the Council during the preceding week, it was necessary for him to make contact with Frizer and Poley (like himself, Walsingham men). Deptford, out of London, was chosen as the meeting place because of the plague epidemic. In this case, Frizer's evidence is true, although the quarrel between the three men went far deeper than a squabble about the bill.

(ii) Frizer's evidence was false, and Marlowe was put out of the way in preference to a formal arrest and a formal charge, which would have been too dangerous once he started defending himself against it. In this case, the long time the men spent together at the Deptford house was necessary to get Marlowe drunk enough to be able to deal with him. Frizer showed only light scalp wounds because he was never in any real danger; he may have given himself a few slashes to make his story more convincing—an old device. The Coroner was so notably incurious because he had been given a quiet hint by someone not to ask too many questions;

he was an official of the Queen's court, amenable to influence from powerful courtiers. In support of this theory, it has been pointed out that medically speaking, Frizer's story is impossible, apart from it being unconvincing on other grounds.

(iii) The Privy Council were prepared to give Marlowe a chance to get away. Deptford was on the river, and Walsingham's men were there to assist his escape. There are no details in the Coroner's Inquest of where and when the body was viewed. Nor is there any evidence of identification. Marlowe in fact need not have been at Deptford at all, and someone else was killed in his place. He did get away, abroad — but if so, his connection with the London theatre was in any case finished.

I was tempted to enter here into an argument about the three theories. But, having decided to present to my readers an imaginative interpretation of a real life story, I will leave what follows to speak for itself. My version of what happened in Deptford and leading up to it, is an attempt to throw more light on the life of Marlowe the double agent, not Marlowe the poet. It is history as it *might* have been.

THE CITY OF CANTERBURY in 1581. One fine September morning a private coach stood outside a small cobbler's shop near the Christchurch Gateway. A young man came out of the house followed by his parents and an elegantly dressed gentleman by the name of Sir Roger Marwood. Briefly and quietly the boy said goodbye to his parents, and there were tears in the woman's eyes as she blessed her son and then shook hands with Sir Roger. A few minutes later the coach had disappeared from sight on its way out of town through the West Gate towards the open country.

Sir Roger, the boy's Godfather, turned to the youngster beside him and said: "Your parents are proud of you, Kit, and so am I. You have chosen a good, humble and secure profession for a boy with your background."

The young man said softly: "Yes, sir," and then turned to look at the Kentish countryside through which they were passing. He had never been away from home before.

Later in the day the coach crossed an open plain, north of London. The road was noticeably more crowded and at last the coach was brought to a standstill by the sheer weight of numbers on the road. The young man looked out and saw then where the people were making for. A short way ahead, silhouetted against the afternoon sky, was a high pair of gallows, around which a huge crowd had already gathered. A bell was ringing dismally, calling others to gather round.

The young man asked Sir Roger for permission to go on ahead to see what was happening. Then he climbed down from the coach and walked towards the gallows. As he

25

came closer he saw that mounted soldiers surrounded the gibbet while foot soldiers kept the crowd back. A cart, with the horse still between the shafts, was drawn up beneath the gibbet and a man, tall and quite composed as a halter was fixed around his neck, stood on the tailboard. He was joined by a younger man, who stood with his eyes closed, lips moving in silent prayer, as another halter was placed over his head. Before the two men, on a second cart, stood a fat chaplain, a local Sheriff and several other officials. The chaplain noisily intoned a prayer while the executioner, standing on a ladder, started to make fast the halters to the cross piece.

"Now is Death over your head," the fat chaplain cried, "and the axe is put to the roots of the tree. Repent you truly of your trespasses against the sacred person of the Queen, her State and her Government. Now is the time of your rising to God, or your falling into everlasting darkness."

The young man from the coach worked his way through to the front rank of the crowd. He stared up at the well-fed priest. Beside him a scruffy tramp passed his tongue round his lips, and further away an old man shook his head in honest doubt as to the rightness of what was going on, while a richly-dressed and moustached merchant nearby nodded his head in the certainty that all was well with the world. The young man glanced quizzically at the merchant's assured face.

The prayer, beseeching the men on the gallows to repent their sins, came to an end and the crowd grew quieter. A few women crossed themselves; two men exchanged smiles; others felt a hard lump in their throats; a man wiped the back of his hand slowly across his mouth. What was happening was just—but many felt a scruple. The fat chaplain finished his performance and looked over the crowd, like a star actor at the final curtain. His glance fell on a mounted gentleman, PHELIPPES, who was sitting on horseback—at the side of the gibbet, and was obviously in charge of proceedings.

Suddenly a voice called from the crowd: "Father Campion, are you afraid to die?"

The older man on the gallows turned to face the crowd. "It is not death we ever feared," he said. "We are not lords of our own life."

Several voices called out then, more angrily than before. "Death to all traitors! Death to the Catholics!"

"If our religion makes us traitors, we are worthy to be condemned," replied Campion.

Phelippes nodded towards the gallows. The tolling of the bell ceased and the executioner raised his hand to the man holding the horses of the cart on which Campion was standing.

"If you are not traitors, pray for the Queen," shouted a voice.

Campion bowed his head and prayed: "May God preserve her most Excellent Majesty and—"

The horses were whipped into action and the cart plunged forward, cutting short Campion's speech with a sobbing sigh.

The crowd gave a half-hearted cheer and then fell silent again as the executioner stepped forward with a great knife and started carving up the body. Then they reacted even more strongly than they had done before the execution. Only the fat chaplain, watching with a pious expression, almost smiled. The young man, revolted by the sight of blood, broke from the crowd and ran unnoticed through the traders' tents and stalls until he reached the shelter of some trees, where he stood, panting and retching. Behind him the crowd continued to gasp in evil fascination.

After a few moments he was aware of a figure beside him, and looking up saw a long-haired old man wearing a brimmed hat and carrying a square basket of apples and pears.

"I see you come away," said the old man. "Oh, it can be a dirty game — religion, I mean. Under Mary they killed the Protestants. Before that — under Henry *that* was — they killed the Puritans and Catholics; Now it's the Catholics again. A dirty game for sure. Apple or pear, Sir? Go good on an empty stomach."

The young man shook his head and then walked towards the waiting coach, which a few moments later was rolling quickly away across the plain, past a signpost which read "Cambridge — 40 miles" and on out of sight. . . .

The University of Cambridge at that time consisted of fourteen colleges and about seventeen hundred students. Wealthy students and the sons of noblemen entered as "fellow commoners". But the bulk of the students were pensioners and the poorest were "sizars" who worked their way through college by doing boot-cleaning, waiting at table and other menial tasks.

Sir Roger Marwood arrived at Corpus Christi College with the young man who had travelled with him from Canterbury. A tutor, MASTER RIDDALL, seedy, forty and rather deaf, approached to meet them, but with his attention all the time on a departing, gorgeously dressed youth to whom he bowed. Then he turned quickly to Sir Roger's companion.

"You should bow, sir," he said.

"Why, sir?" asked the young man.

"Yes, you, sir," replied the deaf Riddall. "When you meet people like the Earl of Essex you should bow. Dr. Norgate is expecting you."

The young man, however, turned to watch as the EARL OF ESSEX crossed to where a servant was waiting with two white horses. They mounted and rode out of the court. As they passed through the gate a group of students made way

for them, bowing as they went by. The young man smiled sadly to himself—he'd never ride out of college on a white horse!

Master Riddall led the way across the court towards Dr. Norgate's house, where they were shown into a well-furnished and comfortable study where DR. ROBERT NORGATE, a man of about fifty, was standing in front of a bright fire. He was the head of the college.

Riddall announced the new arrival: "The Archbishop Parker scholar from Canterbury, Master Christopher Marlowe."

Norgate nodded his head in acknowledgement and briefly explained the principles of college life to the new student, who had come to begin his studies for the priesthood. "A good religious background is worth a great deal in these dangerous days. Master Riddall, here, your tutor and moral councillor, will do his best to guide you for the next three years. This college serves the Queen and the State of England—and if—there is one weak link the—er—chain—you understand?"

"Yes, sir," replied Marlowe. "You need a new link."

"Quite. You may go now."

Marlowe bowed, said goodbye to Sir Roger and went out of the room.

"These scholarship men must be helped, Riddall, but—controlled," commented Norgate. "Discipline is what they need."

"He'll get it here," Riddall assured Sir Roger.

Marlowe was searching for his room in one of the college buildings when he bumped into ROBERT BARNEY, a pleasantly good-looking young man, whose aristocratic background gave him assurance without making him patronizing. Barney introduced himself and led Marlowe up a flight of stairs to an old storeroom at the top of the house. The room was big, dark, bare and cold. There was no fire-place. Four trundle-beds on wheels occupied most of the room, while in one corner a narrow fourposter with curtains obviously belonged to Master Riddall. As they entered, three young men, trotting slowly around the room, looked up expectantly. It seemed that they were playing a form of "follow my leader" in order to keep warm. At the back of the line was JOHN GAGE, a very young-looking student with a friendly disposition. BENJAMIN BULL, the leader, was broad and far better-off than the others and consequently the self-appointed boss. The third student, PETER WATKIN, was thin and poor and a crony of Bull's.

"Are you the new corpse?" asked Bull. "Welcome to the family vault. We who are already dead salute you."

Marlowe introduced himself.

"Do you have any money?" asked John Gage.

"Shilling a week scholarship."

"But your father sends you some," said Bull hopefully.

"My father's a shoemaker," replied Marlowe, "he is poor."

"How absolutely soul-destroying," commented Bull.

The others collapsed into fits of laughter. Marlowe looked rather hurt and John Gage, noticing this, offered to help him make up his bed. Bull and Watkin stood watching them.

"This bed is in an interesting position," remarked Bull. "It receives the full force of the wind that drives under the door."

"The late occupant used to find the nights very refreshing," commented Watkin.

"And who was the late occupant?" asked Marlowe.

"No matter," said Bull strangely. "He has gone."

"Gone?"

"Gone."

They quickly changed the subject by telling Marlowe

that he would also get the full force of Riddall's snoring.
To demonstrate they jumped onto the fourposter. But as
they lay there snoring loudly, the door opened and Riddall
entered the room. He rushed across to the bed, grabbed his
cane and started chasing them round the room, beating
them whenever he could. Suddenly Marlowe was in the way
and Riddall lashed out with his whip—a red trickle of
blood appeared between Marlowe's eyes as he and the tutor
glared angrily at each other. The other boys stopped
running and waited for something to happen. But the spell
was broken by the sound of a gong calling them to supper.

"Open the door for me, Marlowe," ordered Riddall.

Marlowe paused, then went slowly to the door and
opened it. Riddall smirked and walked quickly out of the
room.

*   *   *

London, under Queen Elizabeth, was a frightened city.
Frightened of war with Spain and an attack from the
North by Mary, Queen of Scots. Elizabeth had been slow to
believe that any of her Catholic subjects were traitors and
that missionaries of a new and formidable type had begun
to slip into the country. These were the Jesuits. Fanatics
dedicated to re-establishing the Catholic faith. But their
movements were being carefully watched by Her Majesty's
secret police.

In a spacious but simply furnished room in the Palace of
Whitehall, the Queen's Privy Council sat for long hours
discussing the fight against the Catholics. The Council
included The Lord Admiral, The Archbishop of Canterbury and the Lord Keeper of the Great Seal. The
proceedings were dominated by the Queen's Secretary and
principal minister, LORD BURGHLEY, worldly-wise and quite
relaxed. On his right sat SIR FRANCIS WALSINGHAM, meticu-

lous, conscientious, genuinely religious and the head of Queen Elizabeth's secret police. The topic of conversation was always the Catholics.

"With charity and patience," commented the Archbishop, "we will gather them all to the fold."

Walsingham looked up sharply. "With due respect, my Lord Archbishop, it was not charity and patience that unmasked these last conspirators. It was my intelligence service, paid for by sovereigns from my own coffers."

At this moment a court official entered the room and announced the arrival of Phelippes. Phelippes came forward, bowed low and informed the council that Campion and his Catholic traitors were dead. The Council breathed a sigh of relief. Burghley turned to Walsingham. "You have done the State a great service, Walsingham. Your vigilance has delivered us from evil."

"You speak as though the danger were passed, my Lord," replied Walsingham. "We have only exposed the leaders; we have not destroyed the mission." He added dryly: "Thanks to the Queen's tender woman's heart, Mary so-called Queen of Scots still lives, and with her the hope of Catholic rebellion."

Burghley's voice was equally dry: "On the other hand *we* do not hope for a Catholic rebellion simply for the pleasure of putting it down. And if the Queen executes Mary, there *will* be rebellion all right."

"You are pleased to be facetious, Lord Burghley."

Burghley ignored the remark and asked: "What do you propose as the next stage?"

Walsingham hesitated, then leant forward across the table and spoke forcefully, the plan already clear in his mind: "I propose to intensify my intelligence system on a threefold plan. First, to prevent any more missionary priests arriving in the country from the English-Catholic centres abroad—from Rheims in particular; second, to place my men in Mary's retinue; third—and with your permission, my Lord—to keep closer watch on the universities. They are the breeding grounds of unrest."

Burghley pretended shock: "Our universities?"

"I must remind you that Campion was an Oxford man."

Burghley nodded slowly and smiled: "Speaking as Chancellor of Cambridge I'd say: small wonder."

They laughed and the others joined in uneasily.

*   *   *

The following week Marlowe's college walked in procession to chapel. Marlowe brought up the rear with John, both of them carrying their books and chanting a psalm which echoed back from the chapel where the choir was already installed. Suddenly Marlowe turned his head as he heard other music. It grew louder and then round a corner of the street came a procession of players, marching, tumbling, juggling to a fast jig played on flutes, fiddles, drums and tambourines. Behind them a horse-drawn cart carried their stage properties.

As the two processions and their music met and passed each other in opposite directions, Marlowe slipped into the crowd which thronged the street and then followed the players to a local inn called "The Saracen's Head". The courtyard of the inn, with two galleries running round three of its walls, made an ideal theatre. Marlowe stood and watched.

That evening, when the students had finished their studies, they returned to their room to discuss Marlowe's disappearance.

"And in the first week of term," said Watkin.

"Just as well it was," retorted Bull. "Nobody noticed in the chaos."

He sat on Marlowe's bed and quite openly started

searching through his papers. He suddenly handed the others a sheet with some writing on it.

"Look at this," he said. The others gathered round, read the paper and started to laugh.

Meanwhile Marlowe was standing on the stage at the inn talking with a group of players.

"The public want something new," said the manager.

"This is new," said Marlowe. "It's about the massacre on St. Bartholomew's Day only a few years ago. All the Protestants in Paris were slaughtered."

"Who wrote this rubbish anyway?" asked the manager.

"I did," replied Marlowe angrily.

One of the players came forward and took the script.

"This Duke of Guise," he said after a few moments, "what does he stand for?"

"Himself."

"He can't do that. He must stand for right or wrong. Nobody can play a man who doesn't stand for right or wrong. You must choose."

"Why? Each man for himself! But it's quite clear whose side he's on when the spy comes to him — like this — 'Enter a Spy'." He demonstrates.

"Spies don't enter like that. They enter like this." He makes a cloak-and-dagger entrance. "If they don't, how do you know they are spies?"

"What do you know about writing anyway?" asked the manager. "Let alone about spies, or women, or Catholics. Go away and learn. Then grow a beard and write a play that is a play."

Amid jeering and hand-clapping Marlowe was forced to leave the stage. Only a servant boy, watching him from one of the balconies, felt sorry.

When Marlowe reached his room the other students were already in bed. As soon as he saw him Bull started quoting

a piece of Marlowe's poetry: "Who ever loved that loved not at first sight." Marlowe looked up angrily but John Gage stopped him from going for Bull. "I'm sorry, Kit," he said. "We read some of your papers. There's not much privacy here."

"That's all right," said Marlowe glibly. "I've read some of yours. You're a Catholic. I can deliver you to torture tomorrow."

Before Gage could react Riddall appeared in the doorway and called, "Lights out." The candles were snuffed and as Riddall climbed into bed and almost immediately started to snore, Bull and Watkin pulled the blankets over their heads. But John Gage, still sitting up in bed, screwed up a small piece of paper and threw it to Marlowe, who opened it out and read it. It was a printed leaflet headed: "A Prayer for the Faithful English Catholics." And at the top in ink were the words: "For J.G."

It was some time before Marlowe had a chance to discuss Catholicism with John. A fog of intrigue cloaked the learned rooms and the groups of cold, undernourished young men, who had lived on the same staircase for years, dared not communicate beyond a pale smile. A strong sense of terror reigned everywhere. Finally they found themselves alone in the library. As they talked they pretended to read the library books which were chained to the tables. Robert Barney, who was also present, asked Marlowe quietly if he was sure he wanted to come to one of their secret Catholic meetings. Marlowe replied that he was not.

"You're afraid," said John. "I don't blame you. You can get a year's imprisonment or even be burned at the stake if you are seen."

"Nobody gets burned at the stake for that," said Marlowe.

"They are burning somebody tomorrow on the road to Norwich," answered Robert.

"Who?" asked Marlowe.

"The boy who slept in your bed. High treason."

"What do I care?" Marlowe shrugged the episode aside.

Next day, at dusk, FRANCIS KETT, late of Corpus Christi College, was burned at the stake for Protestant unorthodoxies that the realm could ill afford to have ventilated at this stage of its struggle. And amongst the crowd was Marlowe.

Once more he watched a pious priest blessing the "traitor" and calling him to repentance. Once more he was sickened by the sight of death. The putrid smell of burning flesh made his stomach heave, and in sudden anger he picked up a handful of pies from one of the many stalls round the stake and threw them at the priest.

They hit the man full in the face and immediately the soldiers started pushing through the crowd looking for the culprit. Marlowe ducked away and ran as fast as he could from the commotion.

*　　　*　　　*

As the days gave way to weeks and the weeks to months, feelings in Cambridge began to run higher and higher. But Marlowe kept very much to himself and—strange as it may seem—was soon making his first visit to a Catholic Mass in a private house on the outskirts of town, owned by Sir Arthur Blount. The approach to the house was through a dark wood, many different routes being used by the collection of young men that attended the Mass. Marlowe and Robert and John were introduced in turn to a formidable looking Army Officer by the name of BALLARD.

"Our honoured guest," explained SIR ARTHUR to the

assembled company, "is Father Ballard from the English Catholic College at Rheims."

"I hope," commented Ballard, "that Walsingham does not disguise any of his spies as Cambridge scholars."

The young men laughed nervously.

"You can be sure you are among friends, sir," John Gage assured him.

"Good," said Ballard. "Faithful friends have rescued me from prison and protected my journey through the country. In many ways our organisation is better than Walsingham's but he still thinks he can crush us or root us out. And so he can, if each man is not prepared to give his life in obedience to his superiors — unquestioning obedience, do you understand?"

The young men murmured their approval.

"Only then will the faith endure. There is no choice. As to the counter-attack upon our persecutors — leave that in the hands of those most suited to the work. But if you are called to it — obey."

Without more ado he lead the young men into the small secret Chapel, where they took their places ready for the service. Marlowe looked about him. He could see the large candle-lit crucifix, dancing and flickering in front of his eyes and he felt curiously nervous and out of place.

At the end of the service the young men slipped away to college by separate routes. But as Marlowe left the wood surrounding the house he did not notice a shadowy figure hidden among the trees. After he had passed, the small, beetle-like character emerged from the shadows and stood in the moonlight, looking after him. . . .

Marlowe continued with his studies for a priesthood. He finished his written exams long before the other students, entered for many sports and usually won them. He still visited the house in the woods to hear Catholic Mass and then surprised John one evening on the way back to college by saying: "They are all good, believing, pious people. They have committed no sin in their lives, have they? I don't belong to you 'believers'."

"Don't you believe in us?" asked John. "God is merciful, He—"

"God doesn't realise the difficulties involved."

"You talk as if—" John stopped suddenly and then smiled. "You know, the trouble is you don't trust God enough. He would make things much easier for you if you did."

"Would He?" asked Marlowe. "That's not the way He always works. We keep hearing about His successes. We don't hear so much about His failures. . . . I can't forget poor Kett. Mad religionist they called him. The phrase is neat. Mad—because he dared speak living truth. Yes, that is madness in these erring days. You know what this madness cost him? They burnt him—living—and I saw it. Red flames . . . I can hear his shrieks . . . and I'll never forget the faces all around him with blood-lust written all over them. They burnt him and gained what? Why, a new martyr! A year from now they will be declaring him a saint, these blind worms who have destroyed him, because he preferred to worship God in his own sweet way, without trumped-up sermons, prescribed by fawning, petty prelates of the court! . . . 'Trumped-up sermons. prescribed by fawning, petty prelates of the Court' . . . It's a good line. I must note it down. . . . Let's go our separate ways."

But John was unwilling to finish the argument so quickly. "Tell me, Kit, what do you believe in?" he asked fiercely.

"Have *you* seen a man burn—or hung, drawn and quartered? *I* have—and in the name of God. They are using God in order to use us—to keep us afraid. But I won't be used by them—by those 'set in authority over us'.

Authority! They rule with their money bags. Money, money, money! I'll get money one day!"

"Is that what you want?" asked John. "Money?"

"Yes," was Marlowe's answer. They separated then, John returning to college, Marlowe going to the Saracen's Head, where the players were staying. As he entered, he found a lute player arguing with the stage manager about a new song.

"Get me pen and paper," said Marlowe. "I'll give you a song."

The lute player was not convinced.

"I have the first verse down already," said Marlowe. "I only have to write the rest."

"But it won't be the same measure."

"It will," Marlowe assured him and set about writing. As he did so the other players gathered round, the manager among them. Jim, the servant-boy who had been present at Marlowe's first meeting with the players, also watched.

"Come live with me and be my love
And we will all the pleasures prove . . . "

"Not bad," commented the manager. "You're learning."

"How does the rest go?" asked the lute player as Marlowe scribbled on another sheet of paper. Marlowe handed the script to Jim and asked him to read it.

"I can't read," confessed Jim.

One of the theatre players took the paper instead and the lute player strummed a melody.

"And we will all the pleasures prove
That hills and valleys, dales and fields
Wood or steepy mountain yields.
And we will sit upon the rocks
Seeing the shepherds feed their flocks
By shallow rivers, to whose falls
Melodious birds sing madrigals."

While they were thus engrossed, a man emerged from

the shadows outside the inn and moved towards the window to watch the meeting. It was the ugly, disfigured face with large intelligent eyes of "the beetle".

Jim listened intently to the poem, his eyes fixed on Marlowe's face, and then asked softly if he really was Kit Marlowe.

"What do you know of him?" asked Marlowe.

"Nothing," he said, and turned and went out towards the taproom. Marlowe waited a moment and then followed him. From the taproom some steps led upstairs and soon he was standing outside what he guessed must be Jim's room. He quietly opened the door and found Jim standing by the window, lost in thought. Jim looked round then, a little surprised.

"I've come to tell you about Kit Marlowe."

Jim smiled quickly and rather nervously said that he did in fact know who he was.

"I'm writing a new play called Tamburlaine," said Marlowe, moving towards Jim. "Tamburlaine was a great Persian Emperor. Listen to this:

'I'll ride in golden armour like the sun;
And in my helm a triple plume shall spring.
Spangled with diamonds, dancing in the air
To note me Emperor of the three-fold world'

And so on. I'll need a good actor for it. . . . What is your name?"

Jim told him his name.

"What other names have you?"

"None," replied Jim.

"Who is your father?" asked Marlowe.

"I don't know my parents."

"No parents? I am sorry." Marlowe kept looking at the boy. "There is something in your face which tells of something in your heart to cause you sadness."

"It is as you say." Jim smiled. "But has not everyone

44

some . . . pain inside, some cross to bear, be they young or old, rich or poor?"

It was Marlowe's turn to smile: "Jim, you have wisdom far beyond your years. You philosophize as one who knows."

"I know nothing," said Jim, strangely attracted by Marlowe.

"Nothing at all?" asked Marlowe. "I'll teach you to read. Don't you know any reading at all?"

"Nothing."

The innkeeper suddenly appeared in the doorway.

"That's right—nothing. And not in my tavern, you don't—and not in my time. Out!"

He was a powerful man and had no difficulty in lifting Marlowe bodily from the room and down the back stairs, and propelling him out into the dark night.

Marlowe landed on the ground with a heavy thump, lay still for a moment and then rose and found himself looking into the taunting face of "the beetle".

BEETLE, his eyes on Marlowe's, slowly raised his right arm as if to shake him by the hand, but with a quick violent twist he suddenly seized Marlowe and swung him round backwards so that his right arm was held across his own throat. In that position Beetle forced him away from the Inn towards a garden wall. Marlowe tried to kick backwards, but Beetle pulled on his arm and forced him further over until he began to give at the knees. As he did so, Beetle suddenly let go and Marlowe staggered and fell back against the wall.

"I will teach you that hold. It may come in useful," said Beetle. "It is an effective way of commanding respect."

"What do you want?" asked Marlowe.

"Company—down the road—perhaps," said Beetle.

Marlowe, puzzled, began walking slowly with him.

"University?" asked Beetle.

"Possibly."

"How are your Catholic friends?"

Marlowe stopped walking abruptly. "Who are you?" he asked.

"They call me—Beetle."

"Who are—they?" asked Marlowe suspiciously.

"The people I work for. Important people—who pay well. Does Dr. Norgate know you go to meetings in Catholic houses?"

Marlowe looked at the ugly little man for a long time, his face showing fear as well as fascination.

"You are a spy," he said finally.

"Of course—can't you see?" said Beetle. "I can look in two directions at once, hang upside down from the rafters like a bat. But I pay for facts—for names and places."

"I don't need that kind of money," remarked Marlowe.

"There is only one kind," retorted Beetle.

"How do you become a spy?" asked Marlowe, after a moment's pause.

"There are two easy stages. This is the first," said Beetle, pressing two coins into Marlowe's hand. "The second: You just do it on your own flat feet."

Beetle took him by the arm. Marlowe did not resist and allowed himself to be led away towards the town.

*   *   *

A few days later John Gage was surprised to find Marlowe packing a small bag and naturally asked where his friend was going.

"London," answered Marlowe. "Just for the night. Don't tell the others. Riddall won't notice—nobody will know if you keep quiet."

"London?" John looked puzzled.

"That's where the money lies."

46

"But Kit, you're a student at Cambridge University, surely that's more important than money," said John. "What will you do in London?"

Marlowe ignored his question.

"If you had a golden sovereign," he said, "what would you do with it?"

"I don't know—it's a lot. I'd have to think about it."

"Then think," said Marlowe and tossed him one of the coins Beetle had given him.

"What kind of money is this?" asked the amazed John.

"There is only one kind," replied his friend.

In London, Beetle and Marlowe arrived at Walsingham's house where Marlowe was handed over to a servant called FRIZER, who told him to wait in the hall while he informed Sir Francis of his arrival.

Walsingham was questioning a man called POLEY—a big, shifty and uneducated character with a certain basic courage.

"Would you have carried these letters to Mary?" asked Walsingham.

"No, Sir Francis, I promise you. I was going to put them into your hands."

"Your mission, of course, was to re-open communications between the exiled Queen of Scots and her agents in Paris?"

"Yes."

"Mary's agents evidently have some confidence in you."

"They know me as a staunch Catholic. I hope it may be of service to you, sir."

"To whom were you to carry these letters?"

"To the French Ambassador in London. He'd send them on to Paris, using the diplomatic bag."

"That arrangement will do very well," nodded Walsingham. "We will adhere to it."

"You mean I am to go on acting for Mary?" asked Poley incredulously.

"Naturally. But the line of communication will, in future, be through Mr. Phelippes. We will keep these letters in the mean time and let you know what their information is worth."

"Oh, it's not for the money, sir."

"It is," said Walsingham. "It's the only language I can trust. We will contact you later."

Poley was shown out by Phelippes and when he had gone Frizer informed Walsingham of Marlowe's arrival.

Marlowe and Poley saw each other in the ante-room but took no notice. Marlowe did, however, recognize Phelippes from Campion's execution, but made no mention of it. When Phelippes returned, Marlowe was shown into Walsingham's study and quietly announced: "The divinity student from Cambridge."

An hour later Marlowe was taken to a room where he was to spend the night pending Walsingham's decision on the information he had given him. Marlowe wondered what would happen. It had been quite an experience talking to old Sir Francis himself. He started unpacking his clothes and was about to change when he heard music drifting along the corridor towards his room and a woman's voice reciting poetry. He went out and along the corridor until he found an open door through which he could see into a Music Room where an attractive young woman was sitting on a silver throne placed in the centre of a small stage. She wore a long white classical gown, ribbons in her hair, and was holding a beautiful silver mask before her face. The music was coming from a hidden virginal. Marlowe stopped and listened. The young woman continued to talk to the apparently empty room:

"Queen and huntress chaste and fair
Now the sun is laid to sleep

Diana, in her silver chair
State in wonted manner keep. . . ."

She suddenly stopped as though she had forgotten her lines and removed the mask from her face. As she did so, she saw Marlowe in the doorway and their eyes held one another for a brief moment, then an unseen voice prompted her to recite again and she placed the mask over her face and went on. . . .

That evening Marlowe was introduced to the young lady at a ball and was surprised to discover that she was Walsingham's daughter, FRANCES.

"Do you dance as well as write, Mr. Marlowe?" she asked on being introduced.

"I'm afraid not," said Marlowe.

"Then I will teach you." And she led him onto the dance floor.

"I am writing a play called Tamburlaine," Marlowe told her. "It's about a King and a Queen. The Queen is beautiful and disdainful and passionate. She sits on a silver throne, dressed in a long flowing gown, with ribbons in her hair — like you — this afternoon."

Meanwhile Frizer and Phelippes were searching Marlowe's room. They discovered a few pamphlets and papers and then hurriedly left. . . .

"And what is your poetry about?" asked Frances.

"It's about men and women who love like gods," replied Marlowe.

"And how do gods love?"

"Like men and women."

"Do I dance as well as a goddess?" asked Frances flirtatiously.

"How can I tell?" replied Marlowe. "You are the first goddess I have met. The Goddess Diana."

"Oh, I don't think Diana was married, was she?" said Frances. "Still, Philip — my husband — writes poetry too.

51

He's Sir Philip Sydney—you must have heard of him. He's away on army duties in the Netherlands. He's always away—and I am always very lonely. I hope you will meet him some day."

Before Marlowe could reply he saw Frizer beckoning him from the other side of the room. He excused himself from Frances' presence.

Walsingham was sitting at a desk in his study, ready for their second meeting. He did not look up as Marlowe was shown in. "I have studied your information with great interest and I am wondering if it is entirely accurate," he said.

Marlowe did not try to speak.

"I cannot feel that one who cringes to authority as much as Master Riddall is a Catholic sympathiser. Nor Mr. Bull, whose fortune depends upon a monopoly granted by the Queen. I am sorry to say you face twelve years imprisonment. One for attending a Catholic Mass—and eleven for lying to me."

"What if I was not lying—but just feeling my way."

"The man who gave you the prayer for the Faithful English Catholics—who's he? The same who signs his note J.G.?"

Marlowe reacted then, realizing that his luggage had been searched. But Walsingham went on: "That would be either Jonathan Gatwick or John Gage, wouldn't it? R.B. on the other hand, is obviously Robert Barney?"

"Obviously," murmured Marlowe.

"Who else did you meet at the Catholic house?" asked Walsingham.

Marlowe did not reply. Suddenly Phelippes, who had been standing at the side of the room, took his dagger from his belt, walked over to Marlowe and struck him across the throat. The stinging blow sent the young man crashing back against the wall, where Phelippes stood over him, the knife poised in his hand.

"A priest called Father Ballard," said Marlowe slowly.

Walsingham and Phelippes exchanged glances.

"You have suddenly become very important, Mr. Marlowe. You will be rewarded accordingly and can now— I think—be relied upon accordingly," said Walsingham smugly.

"Because of the reward?" asked Marlowe.

"Not in your case. But because if you betray us, we can betray you—and Ballard's friends are very rough if they are frightened—much rougher than we are, I can assure you."

Marlowe got slowly to his feet, his hand nursing the stinging wound on his throat. "I understand," he said.

"I knew you would. Where is Ballard now?"

"He has gone to hide with Catholics in the North. He is disguised as an Army officer."

"Does he intend returning to the house?"

"Yes. When it is safe to cross to France again."

"Good. He has escaped us once. He shall not do so again."

Phelippes moved towards a side door and disappeared into a small private chamber. When he returned he was carrying a purse of money.

"There are the expenses for your journey and more for your information," he said, handing Marlowe the gold. "Beetle will act as your go-between and bring you any instructions from us."

Walsingham held out his hand and smiled amiably.

"Good luck, Mr. Marlowe. And remember—there are only allies and opponents in this world."

Marlowe, dazed and shaken by the turn of events, left the room in silence. Outside he stood in the corridor wondering what he should do. Before he could decide, however, Frances appeared and asked what was troubling him.

"I must say goodbye, Lady Sydney," Marlowe said quietly.

"Will you come again — and spend some time with me?"

"When it suits me," said Marlowe and walked quickly away.

The following morning Master Riddall was chivying his students out of bed.

"Fifteen minutes," he called to Marlowe as he went out to wash. As soon as he had gone the other boys turned anxiously to one another. Where was Marlowe, they asked. John drew back the covers and revealed a dummy in Marlowe's bed.

"We can't go on covering up for him all day," he said.

"We'll get into trouble ourselves," remarked Bull.

At this moment Riddall returned. "Ten minutes," he said to Marlowe's bed. He dressed and then went out of the room. "Three minutes — and stop sulking." The others breathed a sigh of relief as Riddall finally disappeared.

At breakfast, however, one of the professors asked after Marlowe, noting his absence from the meal table.

"He could have a chill," said Watkin, at the far end of the long table.

"I hear it's a chill," said John, passing the message on.

"He's got a chill," said Bull to his neighbour.

By the time the message reached the professor, Marlowe was definitely in bed with a fever — but was recovering bravely.

It was nightfall before Marlowe in fact reached Cambridge again and his first call was on Robert, who was convinced that his friend really had been ill in bed.

"You must leave college," urged Marlowe. "Tonight, if possible."

"Whatever for?" asked the amazed Robert.

"I've heard that Walsingham's spies know that you and John are Catholics."

"How did you hear this?"

"I heard—I *heard*. That's all. I heard under an oath of secrecy. You must leave at once. Your life depends upon it. I'm going to tell John."

Later that night Marlowe helped the two young men over the college wall.

"You seem to know too much," said John. "I'm frightened for you. You've sold your soul to the devil."

"Don't talk nonsense. Here's some money. Now go."

They embraced quickly and John turned to leave but Marlowe held him back for one brief moment.

"John—a man who sells his soul to the devil, in exchange for knowledge and power—what a play that would make."

John stared at him for a moment, then shook his head in despair and ran off into the darkness. Marlowe returned to his room, took pen and paper and started to write. . . .

It did not take long for Dr. Norgate to discover that Robert and John were absent. He soon called on the other students in Riddall's room and questioned them closely about the matter. Marlowe he addressed particularly sternly.

"In the time you have been with us," he said, "you have not only been a bad influence but have incurred several fines for breach of the regulations."

Marlowe said that he was aware of this, and to Norgate's utter amazement, took a purse from his pocket and handed him a coin. Norgate looked up with affronted surprise, then took the money and left the room without a word. Riddall crossed to Marlowe and stared into his face.

"Where did you get that money?" he asked.

"I've sold my soul to the devil," replied Marlowe. "Now open the door for me. I have work to do!"

He tossed Riddall a coin and the master looked it over as though he had never seen such money in his life before. Marlowe threw him another and with new respect Riddall

opened the door for him. Smiling cynically, Marlowe
stalked out. Back in his room he sat down, picked up his
pen and once more began to write. Long after Riddall had
called the final "Lights Out" he was still sitting there —
brooding over his papers.

*　　　*　　　*

A few months later Marlowe absented himself from
Cambridge again and returned to London — not however to
see Walsingham, but for the opening of his new play,
Tamburlaine, at the Curtain Theatre. It was a roaring
success and Marlowe, delighted and honoured with the
praise he had at last received for his literary work,
addressed his friends in the audience. He found it difficult
to speak at first, but the crowd wanted to hear him.

"I'm moved, I'm drowned, I am ashes . . . I came too
young to this great place called London. My life was calm
enough a life for a young lad . . . before the city and the
theatre swallowed me up. To the theatre! The Curtain!"

The audience cheered: "To the Curtain," they shouted.

Marlowe went on: "My father mends shoes and writes
poetry. A kind of Hans Sachs he is; and mother — my
mother's name is Catherine. I wish she could be here now.
Three cheers to my dears at Canterbury, I beg you!" The
audience cheered once more.

"I look at you — a world in miniature. What a world you
are! Courtiers, poets, sightseers, drunkards. . . . You must
be a goldsmith, sir — you, with the portly paunch. And
here," he pointed to a group of young men, "the Literati:
you weigh the merits of the new stanza — the Petrarchan —
which Wyatt brought from Italy. I thank you specially for
your applause. . . . And who is this burly ruffian? His heart
is bigger than himself: Ben Jonson, my friend. I thank you
for your help, advice, encouragement. And here, standing

among the brawlers, the gamesters, the cut-throats . . . oh, my dear Lord, my cavalier: the Earl of Southampton, friends!" The audience cheered again.

"And here are Green, Donne, Chapman."

He caught sight of a gorgeously dressed youth. "Most exalted Sir!! The delicate, the bejewelled, the exquisite, the bold, peacock-plumed, the emerald-ringed, the ruffled-with-Venetian-lace, the diamond-gartered, R a l e i g h!"

Intoxicated with his own verbal fireworks, Marlowe paused for breath. The audience exploded into applause for him and the popular Sir Walter Raleigh.

"The Queen summons you to write a new play for her, and to read it to her when it is ready," shouted Raleigh. The audience was enraptured.

While Marlowe was celebrating with his friends on the stage after the crowd had gone home, Beetle arrived and informed Marlowe that Walsingham wanted to see him on important business. Marlowe told Beetle curtly to disappear and leave him alone.

*   *   *

Life suddenly seemed much rosier to Marlowe. He spent a lot of time writing, attended more lectures at college and passed many pleasant hours with the boy Jim on the "backs" of the Cam, teaching him to read. Jim was in love with Marlowe but could not help wondering why.

"My black hair and good profile," the poet told him.

"What are you going to do with yourself, Kit?" Jim asked, "when you have your degree—will you be a priest?"

"Would you like that?" asked Marlowe.

"I don't know. It's between you and God."

"Is it?" said Marlowe, looking up to Heaven. After a while he added: "I need your help—above all information."

"Not me, Kit. I told you. I know nothing. I can do

nothing. You too, you've had about as much as you can stand!"

"Look, we were born poor and left to our wits young. We live in a time when the Queen has enemies, when nobles are jealous, when harlots have rivals — a time when a wise man can profit . . . by worming his way into conspiracies; bearing messages, facilitating rendez-vous. I smuggle in weapons and such. Nothing else. I serve either side."

"And you have kept your purse full that way, I know," said Jim accusingly.

"I thought you said you knew nothing," retorted Marlowe sharply.

"I am not as ambitious as you," said Jim.

"I am not as ambitious as the people in London," said Marlowe. "I merely lurk around and skulk and pick up here and there. I don't engage in fanning the fire, in piling on the fuel. They build the fire!"

But Jim shook his head: "Why don't you stick to words. God made you a poet." He turned to look at the pile of papers that Marlowe was working on. "Words are free. Nobody can stop you collecting them."

Marlowe agreed. "They are mysterious things, you know. Take the word God."

"It's a beautiful word," said Jim. "It reminds me of good."

"Now say it backwards," suggested Marlowe, "and see what happens to God."

Jim did so silently and then sat up in horror at what had happened to the word in reverse. Marlowe smiled. "Dog makes me think of the devil," he said. "And talking of the devil. . . ." He looked beyond Jim to where Beetle, partly concealed by the long branches of a willow tree, was standing watching them. Then he got up and joined him.

"Ballard should be here tonight," said Beetle.

"So what?" asked Marlowe. "I've had about as much as I can stand. Didn't I tell you to leave—"

"It's your life," said Beetle. "You know the signal. When the bell rings we get him, dead or alive—or we get *you!*"

Without waiting for Marlowe to reply he slipped away. Marlowe looked after him with a very troubled expression.

That night, at the Catholic house on the outskirts of Cambridge, Ballard was indeed resting on his way south to the coast and to France. The north was apparently holding firm and Ballard would go to Rome to seek the advice of the Jesuit Fathers. Also present at the house were Robert Barney and John Gage—the former anxious to cross with Ballard to France to attend the English Catholic school at Rheims. He explained how Marlowe had saved their lives.

"Where is he anyway," asked John. "He was here a moment ago."

Marlowe was not, however, very far away. Sitting astride a beam in the bell tower, he watched the shadowy forms of many soldiers surrounding the house and wondered whether he could bring himself to ring the bell and jeopardize the lives of his friends. Suddenly he heard footsteps on the loft stairs below and looking down saw the stocky figure of Beetle coming up towards him. In fear and panic he started to ring furiously at the bell. . . .

As soon as the attack on the house had started Marlowe tried to get away in the pitch dark. There was an uproar and shouts of "stop them!" Marlowe collided with two men who drew on one another. The fight was short and bitter. One was killed. Marlowe ran away to the Saracen's Head and to Jim's room.

Jim was already in bed but he let him in and comforted him. Marlowe explained that he had had a "bad dream", a "nightmare". Jim told him that he too had bad dreams sometimes; in his last one Marlowe was in great danger from a stranger, or strangers—he didn't know who—but it was all right in the end. He had saved Marlowe. It was such a vivid dream, that it left him with a feeling of certainty that if ever Marlowe was in danger and he, Jim, was near, God would help him to save his friend.

"You, with your God," sighed Marlowe wearily. "I need a drink . . . badly."

"I'll get some soup—you'll feel better then," Jim said finally.

"No soup! A drink—a drink!" demanded Marlowe. He needed to drown the memory of the last hour.

Jim took a candle and went down into the taproom while Marlowe lay on the bed wondering what had happened to Ballard and the other Catholic supporters and who had been killed. All of a sudden he felt a draught and looked up to see Beetle climbing through the window.

When Jim returned a minute later he found the bedroom empty.

*   *   *

"I see you are not wasting your time," said Walsingham as the jailor unlocked the door of Marlowe's cell.

"I *am* wasting my time here," said Marlowe forcefully, looking up from a table of papers. "Let me go! I was not to blame for Ballard's escape. I played my part."

"I know," said Walsingham. "That's why I've come to release you. But I fear that people like us, Mr. Marlowe, are fated to repair other people's mistakes. And in this case the burden falls upon you."

"How's that?"

"I'm sending you to Rheims—to the English Catholic College."

"Sir, I've had enough, I'm a scholar," protested Marlowe. "I belong at Cambridge. I could never explain my absence."

"I will see to that," Walsingham assured him. "Your orders are to discover the route by which the conspirators enter and leave this country. You do not know our courier but he will know you. Further orders will come through him."

There was a long silence but Marlowe had already seen the hopelessness of the situation.

"And what will be my reward?" he asked.

"Your life — if you return with the information I want," said Walsingham.

Marlowe was trapped — and he knew it.

That evening Marlowe dined at Walsingham's house. After dinner he found himself alone with Frances. "I tried several times to see you while you were . . . in detention, but I was not allowed to," she told him. "You look so serious," she said smiling.

"The life I lead is not all to my liking," replied Marlowe.

"Nor is mine, Mr. Marlowe. At least yours is adventurous. You will sail to the Netherlands in the uniform of an officer, I hear. My husband, who is Governor of Flushing, will arrange for you to continue your journey overland."

"Disguised as a priest," Marlowe added, with a forced lightness.

"May I say how much I admire your courage and devotion to our Queen and Church." Marlowe bowed awkwardly. "My father felt very bad about detaining you in prison. He realises now that you are an exceptional person. I told him so. All I have heard about Mr. Marlowe, I said, makes me respect him more and more: a poet — better than most — facing greater risks without fear and, I am sure, without hatred."

Marlowe listened and wondered what she really thought of him. She was beautiful, young, lonely. He desired her — like one desires to touch a remote star that satisfies by being merely gazed at.

"Mr. Marlowe," said Frances, "when you return from this campaign, I want you to know that you will always be welcome at our house—whenever you wish. My husband, I know, would join me in that. We always think as one. Tell him, should you see him, that his wife presents her love and duty to her husband. And that she wants him to be very, very careful. I don't want him to die a young hero. I am selfish. So tell him to be careful—"

Marlowe replied: "I will tell him his wife is proud of her husband's valour—and to station himself in the forefront of the battle." Before Frances had time to protest, he kissed her on the mouth—then left the room. She stared after him.

*   *   *

Walsingham's spies continued to bring in information, not least among them being Poley. But the strain was beginning to tell on this large and uneducated man. He was afraid that he was being followed wherever he went and thought it dangerous to keep calling at Walsingham's house. But Walsingham's position had been taken over by a younger man—from Cambridge—Lord Essex. He was tall and fair and elegantly dressed and behaved in a much more superior fashion to Walsingham's staff.

One of Poley's letters brought the news that Ballard had safely reached Rome. Phelippes as usual received the letter first. He read it to Essex:

" 'He's there to consult with the English Jesuits. He wants their decision whether it is lawful to assassinate Elizabeth as a heretic Queen. The Spaniard Ambassador in Paris has written to Philip of Spain. Things are coming to a head. Philip is to say whether he will send Spanish military support; the assassination would be the signal for the Catholic uprising. The final decision will be carried in a letter by a young man called Antony Babington.'"

"He's a Catholic land-owner," said Essex. "A protege of Mary's. If she approves the plot we shall get her for high treason. We must double our check."

He began to walk up and down the room excitedly.

"Babington will take his instructions from Ballard," he murmured. "Ballard is in Rome . . . he will naturally return through Rheims—" He paused significantly. "—and in Rheims we have—what's his name?"

"Marlowe," said Phelippes.

While attending the Catholic College in Rheims posing as a Catholic convert, Marlowe spent most of his time trying to persuade the other young priests to read parts in his new play. They rehearsed far into the night, reading in a round room at the top of a tower by the light of flickering candles.

"It will be dawn soon," remarked one of the brothers timidly. "I'm sure the others have been up praying in their cells for an hour or more. Can't we leave this till next time?"

"What is it about anyway?" asked another.

"It's about a man who sells his soul to the devil in return for knowledge and power in this life," said Marlowe.

"And what happens to him in the next?"

"He—er—goes to the Devil," answered Marlowe.

"Oh, I see," said one of the brothers, smiling with relief. "It's a pious work. What's it going to be called?"

"The History of Doctor Faustus."

Before Marlowe could explain further the door of the cell opened and one of the older brothers announced that there was a visitor from England for Marlowe. The other brothers took this opportunity to discontinue the play-reading and slipped away. The courier was from Essex with a message that Marlowe was to wait in Rheims for Ballard.

"Supposing he goes straight to England," complained Marlowe. "I shall be here forever . . . waiting, waiting!"

"Have you found the route yet?" asked the courier.

"No, and I never shall unless—"

"Unless what?"

"Unless I can think of a good reason for going back. Leave it to me."

The courier went away, after wishing Marlowe well, leaving the poet pacing frustratedly up and down his cell. Pictures of the saints smiled down at him from the walls and angrily he turned them over. One slipped to the ground with a crash. Marlowe stared at it for a moment, then gulped down some wine and stalked out of the room and along to Dr. Allan's study. Dr. Allan was the head of the college.

"Yes, my son?" asked the doctor, looking up from some papers.

"May I return to England?" asked Marlowe. "I want to hearten them—tell them how wonderful it is to live in a Catholic country. Give them hope."

"I—"

"Please, Father."

Marlowe did not notice another priest standing at one side of the room, until he turned and spoke.

"He could carry my letter," said the priest.

Marlowe looked round and came face to face with none other than Ballard himself. Ballard, too, recognised him.

"I remember you—from Cambridge," he said. He turned to Dr. Allan then. "This man can be trusted. I could send a copy of the letter with him and half the gold. Does he know the route?"

"No," said Allan. "But don't involve me in your plans. I must know nothing." He stood up and went out of the room. Ballard turned back to Marlowe.

"Our ship sails for Southampton but doesn't off-load.

66

The harbour master is in my pay. He certifies that the vessel is trading down the south coast."

"Where does she go then?" asked Marlowe.

"Straight to London, registered from Southampton — and no one suspects a thing. Take this letter and gold to the Cock Tavern in Fleet Street and ask for Poley. Tell him that the letter is for Babington and is of the utmost urgency. Will you do that?"

Marlowe nodded his head in silence.

"Now repeat the names," said Ballard.

When Marlowe returned to his cell to pack he found Robert Barney there.

"Did you want me?" asked Marlowe.

"I heard a picture fall," said Robert quickly.

"I'm leaving," said Marlowe. "Father Ballard is here. I have an urgent letter to carry to England for him."

"You? For Ballard?" asked Robert.

"For the good of the cause," said Marlowe.

Robert went out then and, a few minutes later, was kneeling in his cell on a prayer stool, praying fervently for Holy guidance.

Marlowe sat on his bunk and counted the money that Ballard had given him. Suddenly he noticed the letter from Essex still lying on the table. Had Robert read it? Would he do such a thing? He jumped up and started packing hurriedly.

Robert, in his room, rose from his prayer. He stood for a long time, then silently went over to Marlowe's door and threw it open. The room was empty. . . .

The ship was already under sail and Marlowe was standing forward in the bows dividing Ballard's money into two parts — one of which he placed in his own purse — when Robert appeared on the empty deck.

"I've found out," he said fiercely. "You're a spy, Kit, for Walsingham. I love you but you must give me that letter."

He plunged at the purse hanging from Marlowe's belt and the two men started fighting. Marlowe managed to push Robert away but as soon as the latter was on his feet he drew a knife and advanced again.

"Then I'll have it from your dead body—" he hissed. "I won't let you take it to Walsingham."

"Fool. I'm acting for Ballard," lied Marlowe.

But Robert plunged forward and there was a swift, bitter struggle for the possession of the knife. Finally Marlowe was driving Robert back, inch by inch, towards the gunwale of the ship. Then suddenly the knife slipped from Robert's hold and Marlowe released his grip.

"Not you, Robert," he panted. "I nearly killed you."

"Kill me if you must," replied Robert, wiping the sweat from his face. "But if you don't—I shall follow you and see that you deliver the letter."

"All right, follow me. But keep away from me when we land; the ports are full of Walsingham's men."

The weather in the Port of London when the ship finally docked from Southampton was windy and dull. Marlowe disembarked as a casual passenger and walked unhurriedly along the wharf, past a row of men fishing from the wall and on towards the City. As he disappeared up the street one of the fishermen turned and looked after him: it was Beetle. He quickly packed up his rod and followed Marlowe out of the docks. Between the two men Robert Barney walked unnoticed.

It was easy to follow Marlowe because he could not walk very fast. The streets were thick with accumulated filth, the mud in the roadway calf high. Pedestrians had trampled a footway past the doors of the tightly packed houses. Only horsemen ventured into the middle of the road. Once Marlowe stopped and looked back casually for Robert. He was surprised to see Beetle and his mouth hardened in controlled anxiety but he made no attempt either to contact or to lose him.

The Cock Tavern was a large and popular inn, well known to all Londoners. Before Marlowe entered he looked round again. Beetle had stopped and was watching him from across the street while Robert was now only a few yards behind, still bent on seeing that Marlowe delivered the letter.

In a small upstairs room Babington and Poley and several other young men — among them John Gage — were drinking and talking excitedly. They were plotting the assassination of Queen Elizabeth.

"Her Majesty Queen Mary has agreed for me to release her from custody myself," announced Babington happily.

"It will be a day of days," said another in rapture.

They drank to the day of days, but suddenly there was a knock at the door and they all grew tense. Poley looked at Babington and then crossed and opened it a few inches. Outside stood Marlowe and behind him Robert Barney was coming up the stairs.

"A letter for Mr. Poley," whispered Marlowe.

"Who from?" asked Poley.

"Ballard."

Poley pulled the door open wider and allowed Marlowe to enter the room. The other young men crowded round as Poley took the letter and handed it to Babington.

"This must be it," he said.

Marlowe saw that Beetle was still waiting in the street when he came down from the upper room, and to disguise the purpose of his visit he seized the nearest waitress round the shoulders and embraced her fiercely sealing her lips with a kiss. Then he ran out into the street, calling that he would see her as arranged that night.

"You got a wench in every tavern?" asked Beetle, coming up behind him.

Marlowe turned and feigned surprise at seeing Beetle in London. Jovially he took his arm in the same grip that Beetle, on their first meeting in Cambridge, had taught him and propelled him away from the Cock Tavern.

"How are you?" he asked. "What are you doing in London?"

"Oh, there were only small fish left in Cambridge. Now I keep an eye open for the big ones in the harbour."

"Hooked any?" asked Marlowe, smiling.

"Well, we didn't expect you so soon."

"My job's finished," said the poet firmly.

"Perhaps it's a good thing. There are changes coming."

"What sort of changes?"

"You'll see — soon enough," said Beetle.

*   *   *

It was raining when Marlowe visited Walsingham. Walsingham seemed much older now — paralysed and grey-haired. Essex was his constant companion.

"Ballard arrived at Rheims three days ago," Marlowe informed them.

"You spoke to him?" asked Essex.

"He recognized me from Cambridge."

"What did he say?"

"He is arriving here shortly. I know the route now. Their ships sail for Southampton but make straight for London registered as trading down the south coast. I came that way."

"I see . . . did he mention any names?" asked Essex.

"Babington — and a man of Babington's called Poley."

"Poley?" asked Walsingham. "Are you sure? He called him a man of Babington's?"

70

"That's what he said."

"Thank you, Marlowe, you have done very well," said
Walsingham. Marlowe, however, said nothing about the
letter he had unwillingly and secretly delivered to the
Catholic conspirators at the Cock Tavern. When he was
finally dismissed he asked for permission to speak to Lady
Sydney. He did not notice the look of anger on Essex's face
as Walsingham gave his consent.

Marlowe went to the familiar Music Room where he
knew Frances always sat. To his surprise she was dressed in
deep mourning and he asked her what had happened.

"My husband was killed — in battle," she whispered. "He
was very brave. Talk, Kit, talk about anything. Not about
me. Tell me what you've been doing."

Marlowe found he could hardly speak. His mind was
racing with the idea that Frances was a widow — and free to
marry again. He had desired her — in a strange, intellectual
sort of way — since the first day he met her, but how could
he — a cobbler's son — ever hope to love her?

"Killed in battle?" he asked incredulously. She nodded.
"He was brave," she whispered.

"I never met him," Marlowe went on. "I want you to
know that. I never gave him your message — any message."

They were looking at each other in silence for a
moment. Then Marlowe heard himself say: "I . . . am so
full of you — my heart and mind is feeling for you all that a
mortal man can."

"I missed you, Kit — Are you well? Tell me about
yourself."

Was there a change in Marlowe, both within himself and
in his dealings with others? He was not insincere, but he
had gained in experience; and although he did not know
for sure that he would dissolve Frances into his arms by
playing gently on her grief, play on it he did. "Oh, I'm just
a stray, lame dog, with rather more scars than most dogs of

my age. You are so young. A girl still. You are too lovely to let yourself die—even a little. Philip wouldn't want you to break yourself over him, I am sure. I am no man like your husband was, but I too would rather sacrifice myself than let you suffer an instant." He held her in his arms. "I would stay with you till your mind was an untroubled calm sea, and your body like a white deer in the forest, a miracle of calm and beauty. Frances, you are worth a man's soul."

He was kissing her hands when Frizer entered the room and asked him to return to Walsingham's study. A few minutes before Poley had arrived and was being closely questioned by Walsingham.

"You have a new master?" asked Walsingham.

"I, sir?" said the surprised Poley.

"You have left us and taken service with Mr. Babington," said Essex.

Poley stared at the two men in open amazement.

"It seems that our guess was correct," continued Essex. "Your new master is plotting with Father Ballard, who is at the moment in Rheims. But you will be seeing him shortly, won't you?"

"I know about Ballard, sir, of course I do; but I haven't heard of him lately—nor of Babington. He seems to be in hiding," Poley lied.

Essex turned to Phelippes. "Arrest him," he said.

Two armed guards sprang forward and seized Poley. As they wheeled him round and started marching him away he saw Marlowe standing in the doorway. He pointed to him excitedly.

"You! So it's you! Filth!" screamed Poley.

Essex moved forward and asked Poley what he was talking about.

"He brought the letter from Ballard," said Poley. "He's one of theirs."

"What letter?" asked Essex, looking at Marlowe.

There was silence in the room as everybody waited for Marlowe to speak. He stepped forward to Poley and looked him over very slowly. Then he turned to Walsingham and smiled.

"I've never seen this man before in my life," he said quietly.

"It's a lie," screamed Poley.

Marlowe struck Poley savagely across the face. "Keep your place, man," he said. Then he turned to Walsingham. "Why should I carry a treasonous letter from Ballard?" he demanded.

"It would certainly not have been very wise, Mr. Marlowe," commented Essex. He looked to Walsingham for a decision on Poley.

"Take him away," said Walsingham. The two guards dragged the struggling Poley out of the room and as he went he screamed at Marlowe still louder.

"I won't forget this, Marlowe. Never. Never. I'll have you."

"What do you do with such people?" asked Marlowe smilingly, when the doors had been closed behind the hysterical man.

"We'll rack him till he talks," said Essex. "And he will talk. He's a spy for money not for a cause. And when he gives names — heads will fall."

As Essex promised, Poley was racked and it was not long before he had revealed the names of every one of Ballard's associates and the exact time of his arrival in the country. Within a few hours an army of soldiers surrounded the Cock Tavern and Babington and his confederates were arrested. Poley continued to talk and the name he shrieked loudest of all was still Marlowe's. This was reported to Walsingham and Essex, but Walsingham trusted the Cambridge poet, whom he had chosen personally as one of his top spies. Babington and his group of conspirators were beheaded.

Marlowe returned to Cambridge, much to the surprise of many of his friends. Most surprised of all were Dr. Norgate and Master Riddall.

"His temerity in returning here takes my breath away," commented Norgate. "Rumour has it that he has lived where no good Protestant Englishman would go."

"There is no smoke without fire," added Riddall.

"I shall quench his fire once and for all. He will never be able to pay the fines he has incurred these past months."

But Marlowe was well able to pay the fines—with a casket of gold sent to him by the Queen, and at the end of term—also at the direction of the Queen—he was gowned and hatted, and presented with a document which read:

"Their Lordships of Her Majesty's Council have thought fit to certify that Christopher Marlowe has never crossed the sea to Rheims but has in all actions behaved himself orderly and discreetly whereby he has done Her Majesty good service."

On leaving the college Marlowe was delighted to see Beetle waiting for him with two white horses. He was unwilling to let himself become involved in any more of the man's underhand activities but he could not help feeling a certain gratitude for his company and present support. As they rode out of the college on the white horses, they were bowed to, as the young Lord Essex had been on Marlowe's first day at Cambridge, and Marlowe could not help feeling that at least the first of his dreams had come true.

* * *

That winter, in London, the famous actor, Mr. Alleyn and his Company started rehearsing Marlowe's new play: Dr. Faustus.

At one of their meetings, Burbage, the manager of the theatre, complained that the play was a risk and he could only offer three pounds for it.

"Four pounds is your usual price," interrupted KYD, a writer friend of Marlowe's. Burbage eventually agreed to pay four pounds and Marlowe watched the rehearsals with a newly found feeling of contentment. It seemed that another of his dreams—success as a playwright—was nearing fulfilment.

"Now that you are in London for good," said Kyd, "would you lodge with me?" Marlowe said he would certainly think about it. He was listening to Alleyn going through a speech with the boy actor playing the part of Helen.

"*Is this the face that launched a thousand ships and*
Burnt the topless towers of Ilium. Oh, sweet Helen—"

"No," shouted Marlowe impatiently. "It's not that sort of a question! It doesn't mean 'is this the face—or is it another face?' It means can I really be looking at it? Can such a wonder be true?"

Alleyn started again: "Is this the face that launched a thousand ships and burnt the towers—"

"Topless towers," interrupted Marlowe. "And with more feeling, Alleyn. That boy is beautiful."

As Alleyn started again Marlowe turned to Beetle and asked: "How much money would I need to marry Frances Sydney?"

"Do you love her?" asked Kyd incredulously.

"I used to think it needed strength not to love anybody," said Marlowe. "Neither woman nor man. I don't think so any more. I need her. . . . Get me some more wine."

"*How comes it then that thou art out of Hell?*" asked Alleyn of Mephistopheles.

"*Why this is hell, nor am I out of it.*"

"It's not a straight comedy line," shouted Marlowe. "It

77

doesn't mean 'laugh, I'm being funny'. It means 'laugh or be afraid'."

"I thought that feeling came more at the end," said Alleyn.

"If you had the slightest shred of understanding," replied Marlowe, "the end of this play would chill your blood."

"Oh, it does," agreed Alleyn. *"My Gahd! My Gahd! Look not so fierce at me."*

"Don't mouth the word God," said Marlowe. "You're playing Doctor Faustus, not the Archbishop of Canterbury's Chaplain."

"The word God has a profound meaning for me," said Alleyn.

"Not for—not for Faustus," shouted Marlowe. "He sold his soul to the devil."

"That's heresy," commented the actor playing Mephistopholes. "The Government—"

"The Government use religion to keep people afraid," said Marlowe. "Now play the fear." He signalled for the actors to continue and then turned back to Kyd and Beetle.

"Yes, Kyd," he said quietly. "I need her."

"You should have stayed in Walsingham's service," said Beetle.

"How could I?" asked Marlowe. "He's dead."

"And you are free—your own master," said Beetle.

"You're right. I have achieved all my ambitions—except one: Frances. And now I am free to achieve her."

"Of course you are," said Beetle cheerfully. "What can stand in your way?"

The prison gates creaked open and Poley came out. Fingering the beard that now massed his thin grey face he stood, blinking up at the weak winter sunshine. His eyes were hollow and red, his body scraggy and bent with

tiredness. He ran his tongue over his rough lips and walked slowly away from the prison. With the death of Mary Queen of Scots the threat against Queen Elizabeth's throne had been defeated and a political pardon granted to all prisoners.

*   *   *

The throne room buzzed with excited anticipation. The Queen had summoned Marlowe to read Faustus to her. The Court — a gorgeous assemblage — was waiting. A group of ladies, their dresses heavily encrusted with jewels, hurried in from the banqueting hall, afraid lest the Queen might already have entered, whilst courtiers, clustered like shimmering stars, talked in impatient whispers: "How can a sovereign of such large gifts, be interested in a play called Faustus — it's supposed to be roaring stuff of blood, despair and cursings"; "They say Marlowe is an atheist and that he was a disciple of the demented Kett,"; "I've heard he lives in the filthiest brothels, the obscurest inns, the rankest dens of pickpockets and ruffians."

Presently a voice announced: "Room for the Queen Elizabeth!" The Queen entered, followed by Sir Walter Raleigh, the Earl of Southampton, Essex, and several others. But not Marlowe. There was an awkward moment when someone explained that the poet had not yet arrived. The Queen, having ascended her throne, surveyed the court sulkily.

"Body of Christ. Somebody say something!" she shouted.

There were a few feeble attempts at conversation and Raleigh once more apologised for Marlowe's absence. The Earl of Southampton had the good idea to start the play-reading without Marlowe.

"He has confided to me portions of the text, your Majesty. It is rather horrifying in some ways, but —"

"Let us hear," said the Queen with interest in her voice.

The Earl began: "The scene is the laboratory of a profound scholar. It is midnight. The old man is omniscient — but not happy. He would gladly forego all knowledge to be young again, to be able to drink and fight and love. He prepares a charm, an incantation that will summon Satan to him from the depth of deepest hell."

There were whispers of "Blasphemy, blasphemy." A few court ladies crossed themselves. One of the men near the throne demanded: "The incantation! Let us hear it!"

"It is in Latin," explained the Earl, "Faustus summons all the fiends." Then he recited:

"Sint mihi dii Acherontis Propitii! Valeat
    numen triplex
Jehovae! Ignei, aerii, aquatani Spiritus,
    Salvete!"

A voice from the door interrupted:

"Per Jehovam, Gehnnam, et consecratum aquam
    quam nunc
Spargo, signumque crucis Quod nunc facio,
    et per vota
Nostra, ipse nunc surgat nobis dicatus
    Mephistophilis!"

All turned, astonished. Marlowe's drunken figure was swaying unsteadily in the doorway.

"I heard you summon Satan. I am here!"

"Are you drunk again, Christopher Marlowe?" said the Queen.

Marlowe pulled himself together. He was crazed with drink but approached the throne as best he could. After he had kissed her hand, he addressed the Queen affectionately: "My dear Lady. No, I am not drunk — but I have been drinking." He spoke with mock gravity. "The drink, the drink. It's killing me. That and late nights. I think my lungs are gone."

He turned to the ladies and gentlemen of the Court. "I am Marlowe, that crawling thing the Gods have not yet blasted, that cur informer everybody hates. I've sent men to doomsday . . . to doomsday—do you hear?"

"Quiet, man, be quiet!" whispered the Earl.

The Queen laughed: "Why do you confess so much? A toast!" she ordered.

The cups were filled and everybody drank to Marlowe—his plays, his poetry. Only Essex watched in silence.

"Sir Walter here has some better poetry than mine," shouted Marlowe.

"Let us hear it," demanded the Queen.

"It is not to be heard. It is to be smoked," said Marlowe mysteriously.

"Smoked poetry?" The Queen frowned. "Whoever heard of such a thing? Now I am sure that you are very drunk. Christopher Marlowe."

Marlowe nudged Raleigh. "Show our Lady! Show them all!"

Raleigh reluctantly drew a packet from his doublet.

"Tobacco!" shouted Marlowe, "Tobacco! Show them!"

There was general talking, whispers and perplexity. "Tobacco?"

The Earl of Southampton called for silence. Marlowe helped Raleigh unsteadily to unfold two huge leaves of the golden weed. Everybody, including the Queen, smelled them. Raleigh explained that tobacco came from the Western shores called Virginia; he found it there some moons ago.

"Fetch me some fire," he said finally. "Now—I roll it like this; I light it—and I smoke it." With studied nonchalance he inhaled deeply.

The crowd watched Raleigh in amazement. "The Spanish call it cigarro," he added. "And now, which of you would like to—smoke?" Several guests tentatively tried—amidst much coughing, choking, giggling and wiping of eyes.

Marlowe, ill and exhausted, lay on the floor—completely forgotten by the Queen and her gathering. Like an opium addict he puffed at his tobacco leaf, producing faint rings of phantom blue smoke. He mumbled: "Is this not better than poetry? London is veiled in fog . . . a deathly blue . . . and grey. I can see nothing. Who's been beheaded . . . sometimes I think I'm mad." He dropped the burning tobacco leaf; it started a small fire and a commotion. Then he fell asleep on the Queen's brocade floor oblivious to the rustle of feather fans and crinolines and the hum of hushed voices.

Essex surveyed the scene with almost leaden gravity; after a contemptuous look at Marlowe he left the room.

*　　*　　*

Marlowe spent a lot of time in Frances' company, most of it riding at the late Sir Frances Walsingham's Estate.

"You are a wild rider," Marlowe told her one day.

"You are a wild poet," answered Frances. "And a sorcerer, they say. A man who is in France and not in France—who is absent and not absent—who moves through the air and is in two places at once. And a blasphemer, too; they even say you believe the earth moves round the sun."

"So it does," said Marlowe.

"So the earth is not the centre of everything," said Frances, mocking him. "Then what about people—are they important at all?"

"You are important—to me," said Marlowe. "I am rich now. Richer than you are. Your father spent all his money on his work."

"He left me provided for," said Frances.

84

Elizabeth

AMERICA

"But he didn't leave you a husband."

"He did," said Frances suddenly. "He arranged a marriage for me."

"Who with?" asked Marlowe in astonishment. "Who with?"

But Frances did not reply. Instead she struck her horse and galloped away across the hard ground towards the house. Marlowe galloped after her, trying desperately to catch up. Was she just teasing him or had her father really arranged a marriage for her? When he reached the house and had stabled his horse he went in to find Frances. He did not notice the crouched figure of a man watching him from behind a wall. It was Poley.

Frances was in her bedroom standing by a great log fire when Marlowe found her. "Who with?" he asked again.

Frances looked at him for a long moment and then said quietly: "The Earl of Essex."

"Essex?" Marlowe could hardly believe his ears.

"I have to, Kit. I have to. You don't know what it's like to be a woman. I need — protection."

"From what? Me? You want protection from Essex against me?" shouted Marlowe angrily.

"Kit, no woman could stay with you. You're — "

Marlowe advanced towards her but she backed slowly away from him across the room.

"You want me to go away?" he asked more quietly. "For ever?"

"Yes."

"Never to see me again?" Then he was shouting again: "Essex. Only Essex?" He grabbed at Frances and drew her towards him — and suddenly she was in his arms and kissing him. It seemed that his last and greatest dream was coming true. . . .

*   *   *

Beetle and Marlowe were staying at Kyd's house. Beetle was acting as man-servant.

"This is no job for me," he complained to Kyd. "After all, I served Sir Frances. I should have got out in time."

He tensed suddenly as he heard the sound of horses outside, and a moment later footsteps on the stairs.

"And that's what I'm going to do now," he hissed, making for an open window.

"What are you doing?" asked the surprised Kyd.

Even as Beetle disappeared, the door of the room burst open and a gang of soldiers rushed in.

"Where's Marlowe?" asked one of them, seizing Kyd.

"I don't know. Let me go," wailed Kyd.

"Whose are these papers?" asked the soldier.

"His, I swear it. He uses my table."

The soldiers started to drag him out of the room.

"I believe in God," screamed Kyd. "I am not responsible for his opinions. I believe in God."

Beetle, no longer the fit man he had been in Cambridge, ran ahead of the soldiers through the cold, muddy streets to warn Marlowe. All around him were houses with barred windows and locked doors, marked with a large cross showing where the plague, the worst killer in history, had suddenly struck.

Marlowe was still busy rehearsing the play.

"It's senseless the way you do it," he complained, leering drunkenly around at the players. A young boy dressed as Helen tried desperately to catch the poet's every word.

"Faustus conjured up the Devil without a twinge of conscience. Faustus was right. There was nothing he could not do. He can achieve Helen. He can gain the whole world."

He signalled for the boy to start the scene again. The boy began to speak his lines and then seemed to get them all mixed up, making nonsense of the verse, and suddenly he fell forward on the stage. The rest of the cast immediately gathered round.

"Don't touch him," warned Mr. Alleyn. "It may be the plague." Marlowe moved forward and straightened the boy up. "Where does he live?" he asked. "We must take him home."

"His father's a shoemaker in the city," said Alleyn.

Marlowe looked at the boy with special affection. Suddenly the boy stirred and opened his eyes. "It's nothing, sir," he whispered. "I'm hungry. I keep fainting. It's nothing — I haven't eaten — that's all."

"Don't you dare faint during the performance," smiled Marlowe. "You'll deserve no applause if you do." He explained that the play had to go on in time. He had worked on it since his student days and he had one wish: to see it staged!

At this moment Beetle burst into the theatre and ran onto the stage.

"They've taken Kyd," he panted to Marlowe. "They're after you. Run!"

Marlowe hesitated. He had known for some time that things were catching up with him — but the play must go on!

"Whatever happens to me," he said quickly to the players, "get the play ready. Promise me — on your honour — that you'll do that."

Already they could hear the sound of horses outside. He looked around at the assembled actors, then bent and picked up the boy in his arms and started walking toward the main entrance.

"Don't go out that way," shouted Beetle. "You're mad."

But Marlowe paid no attention and, fascinated, the company followed him out into the street.

The soldiers had dismounted and were moving to surround the theatre when Marlowe appeared, carrying the boy.

"Stand back," he called in a loud voice. "It's the plague. Do not touch him—these very rags may give you the infection."

The other actors, understanding Marlowe's game, began to shout similar warnings and, as if by magic, the soldiers backed away, leaving a clear path for Marlowe to carry the boy to his horse. He placed the boy's body across the horse, then mounted and suddenly whipped the animal into action. The soldiers, realising that they had been fooled, jumped onto their own horses and galloped after him.

Rats were pouring into the streets of London. Scaly feet pattering on a stone floor. Yellow teeth tearing at wood-work . . . with, now and again, a scream or a shriek. A sickness of the soil was driving blind rats up into the world of men, through cellars, sewers, garbage heaps. . . .

A doctor pulled a sheet over a dead face. From the small room where the dead man lay, the doctor went out into the narrow, crowded street. Someone was painting crosses on the doors. A "tomorrow we die" atmosphere reigned everywhere. Drunk soldiers, bare-breasted women, were howling a song. Inspired by a crazy theory, or religious mania, that flagellation and sexual activity were a pro-tection against the Sickness, men and women were copulat-ing on the roadside. Others were flogging themselves in a graveyard. Bodies that showed distorted limbs and gigantic heads were being carried for burning outside the city walls.

Marlowe's white horse galloped through the narrow street. Marlowe, still holding the boy, jumped off and hid in a doorway. The horse galloped on. A company of soldiers rode past in pursuit. Marlowe said farewell to the boy, then crossed the street and entered a house—a brothel teeming with people.

As Marlowe pauses, panting in the doorway, a pretty young prostitute comes forward quickly and shows him to the stairs that lead to the first floor. From the murky

depths, sailors can be heard singing raucously, girls entwined around their necks. Their noise drowns the sound of the soldiers in the street outside who have turned back puzzled at having found only a riderless horse.

In the upstairs room of the brothel, two women are with Marlowe: the elder is a dead-pan, sleazy, rather good-looking harlot, the other, the pretty young prostitute. Marlowe is looking out of the window. Below in the street he can see that the soldiers have started a rapid house to house search, moving in the direction of the brothel. Two or three detachments of soldiers leap-frog each other, taking every second or third house. A priest can be seen passing by.

"Get the priest!" says Marlowe.

"What, *here?*" asks the harlot.

"Yes!" Marlowe gives her money and she leaves quickly. "I'm dying . . ." says Marlowe, making for the bed.

Down below the soldiers continue their search. As the priest passes by, the harlot intercepts him and leads him to the house. Shortly after the soldiers follow. Inside, they penetrate into the recesses of the downstairs room disturbing the sailors. There are shrieks and giggles. Other soldiers start to climb the stairs.

In the upstairs room Marlowe is lying on the bed, apparently at his last gasp. The priest is with him.

"Father, I am a terrible sinner," whispers Marlowe.

"We are all sinners, my son, and yet we can all be brought to repentance."

"Can we?" Marlowe hears the noise of soldiers' boots clattering up the stairs.

"Come closer, Father. Hear my confession. CLOSER!"

The door opens. Led by the prostitute the soldiers burst into the room. They hesitate at the sight of a dying man receiving his last sacrament from a priest. Marlowe moans.

"He's been lying here all day. He's dying," says the pretty prostitute.

The Priest motions the soldiers to depart. They go; the prostitute closes the door. "Now, my son, confess to thy sins," whispers the Priest with real compassion. Marlowe hears the sounds of the soldiers descending. He grasps the Priest's cassock.

"I have seen both sides of every question; I have run with the hounds and hunted with the hare; I have discovered that two blacks make a black; and that to understand all is to forgive nothing!" He sits up suddenly. "And what have you discovered, Father? That you are a useless old man? You can confess to me. What have you done? Turned your coat? Seduced your neighbour? Filled your belly? Robbed a church?"

The Priest is shocked. "You have a fever, my son. I can be of little use to you if —"

Downstairs the door bangs behind the soldiers.

"You can be of great use to me," says Marlowe threateningly. He jumps up, drawing a dagger. "Take your cassock off. Quick!"

The Priest hesitates. Marlowe pounces on him, twists his arms and starts to tear the cassock off him.

"Arms up — don't move till I tell you!"

The Priest is stripped to his underwear. Marlowe puts on the cassock and makes for the door.

"I'll return your cassock in Heaven — or the other place!" He reaches the door and flings it open. Swords drawn and glistening a large body of soldiers waits motionless on the stairs. The harlot is with them — impassive as ever. Marlowe looks at the Priest and shrugs:

"It'll be the other place. . . ."

*　　　　*　　　　*

In a large, common prison cell, so large that the little

light that filtered in from high windows failed to penetrate its uttermost corners, Marlowe sat, unshaven and dirty. Cobwebs and rats were everywhere. The prisoners, or what could be seen of them, were a motley collection of all ages and classes. Marlowe, still in priests clothing, sat a little apart, near another prisoner.

"I don't know why . . . just got a little drunk . . . I must have said something . . . I've done nothing," the prisoner muttered half to himself.

"I'll see if I can get you released," Marlowe told him.

"You? How?"

"I have friends in high places."

"What are you in for, then?" asked the prisoner.

"Atheism, blasphemy, heresy, piracy, burglary, high treason and lots more."

A Priest, with haggard look and burning eyes, sat nearby. Marlowe seemed to know him.

"*We* have friends in high places, have we not, friar?" asked Marlowe, looking up and pointing a finger to Heaven. "But I bet you are afraid of Hell!"

"I am not as important as that." The Priest's terrible eyes focused on Marlowe. "Hell is for the great. The very great . . . I don't know anyone who is great enough for Hell . . . except Satan."

A prison guard entered on top of the stairway which led down to the prisoners; he unlocked the iron gate.

"Marlowe! You're wanted up top," he announced.

In a spacious room above the prison, the Privy Council sat at a large table in highbacked chairs. The Council included Lord Burghley, the Queen's Secretary, Lord Essex, the Lord Keeper of the Great Seal, the Lord Admiral, the Archbishop of Canterbury, secretaries and guards. Marlowe was escorted in and led to a stand for the accused.

The Lord Keeper spoke first: "Christopher Marlowe, we

are conducting an enquiry as to whether you should stand your trial in the High Court for heresy, blasphemy and atheism".

"Which side am I on?" demanded Marlowe.

"This is what we want to know," said the Lord Admiral.

"How can I know if I have committed heresy until I know which side I am on?" asked Marlowe.

"This is heresy in itself," replied the Lord Admiral.

The Archbishop spoke next: "You are wearing priest's clothing. Did you study for the priesthood?"

"I did. Twice."

"Why twice?"

"Once for each side. Once for you — once for the Catholics. I've seen how it works. I've been a pawn in your game. I've seen the Catholics trying to get back what they have lost — and you trying to keep what you've gained. It's nothing to do with God — only with money and power, power and money, the safety of thrones. . . ."

Essex cut in for the first time: "You are here to answer our questions, not to practise the cheap rhetoric of the theatre."

The Lord Keeper spoke again: "You are reported to have said that all Protestants are 'hypocritical asses'. Is that true?"

"Yes," replied Marlowe, "they are."

The Lord Keeper continued, "The question was —"

Essex interrupted, "You stand by that opinion?"

"I stand by all my opinions," said Marlowe triumphantly.

The Lord Keeper was getting impatient: "My Lords, must we listen —" But the Archbishop interrupted him: "Have you or have you not said that — if God existed — the best religion would be that of the Catholics?"

"Naturally, I prefer their ceremonies, their organ music," said Marlowe, "I like ceremonial and ritual, your Grace. I am a poet. Poets have hungry eyes and hungry ears and hungry senses."

Essex referred to a report in front of him: "You state here that if you were asked to write down a 'new religion', you could greatly improve on the Bible?"

"It's a badly written book, written over 1000 years ago. We are different people today, we know more — we need a new religion — the universe has yielded secret after secret. . . ."

"And what would this new religion be?" asked Lord Burghley.

"Call it what you like. A religion of reason and knowledge and love — not hobgoblin mysteries and ignorance and whips and gibbets."

Essex spoke again: "You have stated before witnesses that Moses was a fraud —"

Marlowe: "And so was Jesus —"

The Lord Keeper jumped to his feet: "My Lord, must we listen to this?"

Marlowe continued: "Religion served its purpose among primitive peoples. Today it's a device of policy — your policy! It has nothing to do with God . . . where is God? If he is not in the hearts of the rulers and the teachers, where is he? If I had known where to look for him, I might have found him . . . I wanted to. . . ."

The room swam before Marlowe's vision. The Privy Council sat silent, staring at their prisoner.

"I am a sorcerer moved through the air by your Lordships. I'm a blasphemer who knows and loves men devoted to killing each other. I am an atheist who has been shown God killing men, and I am a traitor who has seen men killing God. Stand upside down to condemn me, then piously cross your eyes, dot your T's and go home."

He was swaying now in the dock, beads of sweat glistening on his face, his eyes glazed.

The Lord Keeper looked around at the other members of the Council — then he turned back to Marlowe.

"Christopher Marlowe," he said. "We declare that you must stand your trial before the High Court."

"Whatever the verdict, my son," said the Archbishop quietly, "we shall pray for you and if you can, pray for yourself."

"I should pray?" screamed Marlowe. "Who to? To your God or your Saints? I don't believe in your God, who put you where you are, who watches over your stinking prisons and who wants me there too. I don't believe in—"

"Take him away," signalled the Lord Keeper. Two soldiers stepped forward and took Marlowe firmly by the arms. He began to struggle furiously but he was too weak to break away from his escort.

"I don't believe," he screamed. "I don't believe!"

He was taken back to his cell and placed in irons. He continued shouting.

"Let me out. I'll use my influence with Raleigh, with Southampton, the Lady Sydney. Think what that means . . . I am Marlowe! I have written Tamburlaine and Faustus. They are played up and down the country, they are sold in the book-stalls. I am writing Hero and Leander, a great poem, it will make money! I promise you gold! Gold! Be merciful, be just, be human—let me into the streets, let me into the streets!"

Then he collapsed.

There was quiet in the Council Room; the Lord Keeper turned to the others and said: "It is agreed then, my Lords, that we send him for trial without delay?"

"It would be most imprudent," said Burghley quietly. "He'd defend himself and in so doing, he would show that he acted under our protection."

"What do we do then—let him go?"

"Certainly not. If we did that, he would put us all on trial."

"I think that this would be best dealt with unofficially," said Essex.

"You mean that you will release funds to see that he is deported from England?" asked Burghley.

"If that is the Council's wish," said Essex.

"When can you arrange it?" asked the Lord Keeper.

"Immediately," replied Essex.

Outwardly Frances showed little reaction at the news that Marlowe was to be deported. Inwardly, however, she was deeply concerned for him and as she sat scribbling a note, which Essex dictated at his official room in Whitehall, her mind searched frantically for a way to help him. The note, by implying that Frances would join Marlowe in his flight, was designed to draw Marlowe out of London to the docks at Deptford and as proof of the letter's validity Essex removed Frances' favourite locket from her neck, and placed it with the scroll.

"His departure will solve many problems," Essex said. "Before Marlowe realises what has happened he will be on the ship and out of our lives."

"When does he sail? And where from?" asked Frances.

Essex hesitated. "From Deptford—on the next tide." He kissed her. Frances did not try to resist his approaches nor did she encourage them.

Essex watched her ride away from the house in her coach . . . on her way home.

Then he went back inside and down a long corridor to a small room. Poley was waiting there. He threw him a bag of gold. "I want him killed," said Essex coldly. "When and where I don't want to know."

Marlowe lay under a high window in the large cell and looked longingly at the sky. One of the prisoners leered up behind him and laughed.

"So you've got friends in high places, have you?" he said. "But you're back here—just the same."

Marlowe turned round slowly but did not reply. Suddenly the prisoner spat viciously in his face and walked away. Marlowe watched him for a moment and then became aware that he was being addressed by the prison gaoler who was standing in the doorway and trying to attract his attention.

"Master Marlowe? You are free, sir. Please follow me."

Marlowe looked at him incredulously, then, tense and unsure, he followed him out of the cell, leaving the other prisoners staring after in amazement.

Outside, in the Warden's office, Beetle was waiting. "We've got to move quickly," he said. "They may try to kill you."

"Who?" asked Marlowe, rubbing his eyes against the bright light.

"The Council. It could be the old trap—pretend to let you go, then have you done in. The Council's divided, one group against the other. We've got orders from the highest of the high and mighty. I think it's safe."

"How can you be sure?" asked Marlowe.

"You've got a friend—come outside." Beetle led him out into the prison yard where Frizer and a man called Skeres were waiting. Frizer handed Marlowe the letter and locket from Frances.

"My mistress will meet you at the Eleanor Bull's Inn at Deptford. We will take you there."

Marlowe read the letter nervously, then nodded his head in agreement. "You're right," he said, "she's coming." Had Frances really broken with Essex? Or was it a trap?

They helped him onto a horse and a few seconds later they all rode out of the prison and headed towards Deptford.

*   *   *

While he waited for the next tide and Frances' arrival, Marlowe sat with his companions in an upstairs room in Eleanor Bull's Inn. It was a low, long building with the usual fore-court and garden, where already a group of players were setting up a small stage in preparation for a performance of one of their new plays.

"Where is the ship bound for?" asked Marlowe.

"Don't you worry about anything, sir," said Beetle. "Your lady isn't due here till dusk. As soon as she arrives, we'll send Skeres down to find the master. We'll get off tonight."

Marlowe crossed to the window and looked out onto the backyard and the road beyond.

"Don't show yourself," warned Frizer. "You're too well known. If it gets around you're doing a skip, it's all up with us — and you."

Marlowe backed away from the window and sat down on a stool. The waiting was beginning to tell on his nerves.

Frances was in her favourite Music Room, trying to play the spinet. But it was impossible to concentrate and suddenly she banged angrily on the keys, got up and went to call her maid.

"My coach," she said. "Quickly!"

"I'll get some food," said Frizer. He went out, leaving Beetle and Skeres with Marlowe. Outside he listened for the sound of the door being locked behind him. Then he moved along the stone passage, from which several doors led into other rooms, and went down into the yard at the front of the house. It was really a garden with rose bushes and flowers, but now the players were putting finishing touches to the curtains and scenery of a make-shift stage set up in one corner. Some sailors and local people were sitting and standing around talking and drinking. As Frizer walked across the yard, one of the players was showing a paper to a heavy, blousy woman who had a voice like a fog-horn.

"It's a proper license," the player assured her. "We have to live, madam. It's terrible for business, this sickness, with all the London theatres closed."

"I know all about bad business," replied the woman. "As long as you haven't got the plague with you."

She walked away toward the main room of the inn which Frizer had just entered. The room was crowded with sailors and militia men and it was some time before he could see anybody to ask for food. Then he noticed an untidy serving boy handing plates of food to a group of sailors sitting at tables on the far side of the room. He crossed to them.

"My master wants some drinks in the backroom," he said.

The boy looked round and scowled. It was Jim, from Cambridge.

"For how many?" he asked.

"Make it four," said Frizer. "And food. Fried eggs and ham. And—when a lady arrives—and I mean a lady—call me." He went out then.

"Who's his lordship?" asked one of the sailors.

"I dunno. I don't like his face," said Jim.

A few miles away Poley was riding along the coastal road towards Deptford. The fatigue of the afternoon had started to show in his excited face. But he never stopped and rode on steadily.

Marlowe was becoming increasingly impatient.

"Why don't you see about the ship now?" he asked.

"There's plenty of time," said Beetle. "Frizer will go. Besides, I'm not so keen to see you leave. After all, we've been together for quite a while, you and I." He smiled.

At this moment there was a quiet knock at the door. Beetle unlocked it and let in Frizer. "They'll bring some food," he told them.

"When your mistress arrives—" began Marlowe.

"They'll call me—don't worry."

"When she comes—disappear. I want to be alone," Marlowe told them as they started setting the table ready for the meal. Frizer poured out some more drinks and handed one to Marlowe. "It'll quieten your nerves," he said. "We shan't be sorry to get rid of you, sir. Nothing personal—it's just that—"

"What's that noise?" asked Marlowe suddenly.

"Players in the yard," Frizer told him.

Marlowe crossed to the window, keeping to one side and looked out but he could see nothing.

In the passage outside Jim was approaching with a tray of tankards when he heard voices coming from the room.

"I'm going out into the garden," said one.

"You're mad. You'll ruin everything."

"I'll ruin my temper if I stay here much longer. Take your hands off me." There were the sounds of a scuffle and Jim, alarmed, knocked loudly on the door. The heated voices stopped, the door opened a few inches and Frizer peered out.

"Where's the food?" he asked.

"It's cooking—and I haven't got ten hands."

Frizer took the tray and Jim moved away, listened for a moment and then finally went.

Poley rode on through wooded country towards Deptford. Every few miles he met carts and coaches carrying refugees from the London plague to the countryside.

In the room at the inn, Beetle handed Marlowe another drink. The men sat in silence . . . waiting.

Poley arrived at the inn just as it was growing dark. He left his horse in the street and went into the garden. A girl tried to befriend him in the entrance but shrank back as he brushed past her. He looked round the garden and then sat at a table, ordered a drink and asked to speak to the innkeeper.

In the private room at the back of the house Marlowe suddenly stood up and said quietly. "I'm going out into the garden." Frizer leapt to his feet and faced him at the door.

"My orders are to get you away. You'll be seen," he said.

"Who by?" asked Marlowe. "Spies over the garden wall? Get out of my way." Slowly Frizer obeyed. Beetle got up and crossed to Marlowe's side. "I'll come with you," he said and led him out. Frizer followed them, leaving the door open. Skeres looked after them nervously for a few moments and then suddenly jumped at a minor explosion from outside — which sounded like a distant shot.

On the stage in the garden the frightening figure of the Devil appeared dramatically from a theatrical cloud of smoke produced by the explosion.

"Now, Faustus, what would thou have me do?"

A small audience had now gathered round the stage — Some of them standing, some sitting, others lying drunkenly on tables and chairs.

Faustus declaimed:

"I charge thee wait upon me whilst I live
To do whatever Faustus shall command.
Be it to make the moon drop from the spheres.
Or the ocean to o'erwhelm the world
To give me whatsoever I shall ask,
To tell me whatsoever I demand,
To slay my enemies and aid my friends,
And always be obedient to my will."

During this Marlowe and Beetle had come out into the back of the garden and stood listening. Marlowe realised that they were performing his play. He watched, fascinated and delighted. A few yards away, unknown to him, Jim stood, tray in hand, watching the frightening figure of the Devil. Beyond him was Poley.

Marlowe tried to move forward to get a better view of the stage, but Beetle held him back. "You mustn't be seen," he said. They stood quietly in the shadows and continued to watch.

The big blousy woman ordered Jim into action and the boy moved around the garden collecting empty mugs, his eyes still on the stage. A fat, repulsive peasant girl, who looked like an amazon badly in need of a man, tried to force him onto her lap, but he freed himself quickly and made for the main room.

On the stage the young boy actor adjusted his wig and prepared to make his one big speech as "Helen". Marlowe nudged Beetle as he remembered the last time they had seen the boy. He recited his speech without a fault and ended with a great flourish but the audience was not impressed. There was a stony silence. Marlowe, livid at this injustice, began clapping loudly—alone at first until a few others joined in sleepily. The boy bowed proudly, not recognising Marlowe among the crowd of spectators.

Poley glanced up then and saw Marlowe for the first time. He looked round the crowded garden and noticed Frizer leaning out of an upstairs corridor window. He slipped away from his table and walked quickly towards the house. In the doorway he suddenly faced Beetle. Poley motioned him inside. Beetle went, leaving Marlowe to watch his play being performed for the last time before his eyes.

Upstairs in the private room Frizer, Skeres and a half-hearted Beetle faced Poley. They were talking in feverish whispers.

"It's simple," said Poley.

"We'll go to prison," said Frizer.

"That's nothing new. This time you'll be out quickly. It will be self-defence. We'll say he was drunk—started a quarrel—and then you did it. I'll be behind the door. We'll be the only witnesses."

"You pay us first," said Frizer.

"Half now and half later. Now get to your places." He slipped out of the room and back down the stony passageway.

Outside in the garden, some constables had entered the inner yard and Marlowe, seeing them and suspecting the worst, quickly withdrew into the house. He found the other three men upstairs, pretending to play backgammon. There was no sign of Poley.

"Beetle, what will they think of me in London?" asked Marlowe. "Will they think I've lost my nerve?"

Beetle did not answer.

"We shall spread the word that you are dead—of the plague," said Frizer. "Don't worry, you'll soon be forgotten."

"What are we?" said Marlowe in a far-away voice, "a drop in the sea? No, not even that . . . we are—and we are not. . . ." He turned from the window. "How much longer do we have to wait?" he asked impatiently. As he looked round, he caught the glances exchanged between Frizer and Beetle.

"I don't believe there is a ship," he said slowly.

"Go and find your own then," Frizer answered curtly.

"And Frances. She's not coming, is she?"

The men did not reply.

"Which side are you on?" asked Marlowe.

"Does it matter?" said Frizer.

"It does. It does matter, Beetle! *Which side?*"

"My own," said Frizer.

"I'm going back. Get the horses," said Marlowe quickly.

There was a loud clap of thunder from the stage below and suddenly Frizer stood up, his dagger in his hand. Marlowe dashed towards the door, pulled it open—and found himself facing Poley. He began to back across the room.

"*All beasts are happy,*" came Faustus's voice from the yard under the window,

"*For when they die*
   Their souls are soon dissolved in elements,
   But mine must live, still to be plagued in hell.
   Curst be the parents that engendered me."

"What are you doing here? Curse you," said Marlowe to Poley.

"*No, Faustus, curse thyself,*" said Faustus. A clock began to strike in the distance.

"*It strikes,*" screamed Faustus. "*It strikes.*"

Poley, smiling wickedly, began to advance on Marlowe.

"*Now, body turn to air,*" shrieked Faustus,

"*or Lucifer will bear thee quick to hell!*"

A fierce struggle started between Poley and Marlowe. The others stood watching, waiting for a chance to strike. Poley managed to seize Marlowe's arm and suddenly Marlowe's dagger dropped from his hand. Beetle jumped forward and picked it up. For a moment Poley and Marlowe were locked together—motionless—in each other's arms. Marlowe stretched out his fingers towards Beetle for his weapon. Beetle looked quickly from Marlowe to Poley and then—threw the dagger to Poley. Poley lunged and Marlowe fell to the ground, the dagger sticking grotesquely from above his right eye.

Mephistopholes could be heard laughing in the garden.

The four men picked up their knives and other belongings and ran, leaving Marlowe lying on his back in the middle of the room. He tried to crawl towards the door.

"*My God, my God, look not so fierce on me,*" beseeched the doomed Faustus.

Jim, in the kitchen below, picked up a tray of food and carried it upstairs. He did not recognise the blood-covered figure on the floor as his lost friend. He dropped the tray in fright and ran through the passage for help. But out of

111

one of the side-doors, the strong arm of the big, fat
peasant amazon caught him as he flew past. The girl
stopped his protest with her other hand and brutally forced
the choking boy into her room. The door slammed behind
them.

On the stage, now lit by two candles, the players
declared:

"*Cut is the branch that might have grown full straight
And burned is Apollo's laurel bough
That sometime grew within this learned man. . . .*"

Marlowe tried once more to reach the door but the effort
was too great. "God," he whispered — and died, his brain
full of dagger.

There was the clatter of horses' hooves outside as Frances
arrived at the inn. She left the coach and began crossing
quickly through the garden towards the house in search of
Marlowe, her steps quickening in happy anticipation.

Marlowe is dead. A ray of candlelight flickers across
some rats who run over his body. But his play continues in
the background:

"*Faustus is gone, regard his hellish fall,
Whose fiendful fortune may exhort the wise
Only to wonder at unlawful things
Whose deepness does entice such forward wits
To practise more than Heavenly power permits.*"